MONUMENTS MARKING
THE GRAVES OF
THE PRESIDENTS

A COLLECTION OF PHOTOGRAPHS AND INSCRIPTIONS

MONUMENTS MARKING THE GRAVES OF THE PRESIDENTS

By

ARCHIBALD LAIRD

THE CHRISTOPHER PUBLISHING HOUSE
NORTH QUINCY, MASSACHUSETTS 02171

This book is lovingly
dedicated
to my wife

RUTH WASHBURN LAIRD

whose
infinite patience
sympathetic understanding
and
photographic talents
made it possible

ACKNOWLEDGMENTS

To produce a book devoted to the graves of the Presidents of the United States, it was not only necessary to personally visit the graves, take pictures and make copies of the inscriptions, but also to receive the assistance of the officers in charge of the public and private burial grounds.

In one book entitled *Presidential Shrines From Washington to Coolidge,* devoted to birthplaces, homes, and, in a few instances, to the graves of the Presidents, the graves and their monuments were not mentioned in detail. Inscriptions were omitted, or were inaccurate, and only a few monuments were represented by photographs.

This work is devoted exclusively to the graves and monuments marking the graves, with the exception of where public funds were expended by State General Assemblies to erect a memorial to a departed President at the place of his death, or near his last resting place. This situation happened on three occasions: James Monroe died in New York City and rested there for over twenty years; David R. Atchison, President for one day, Plattsburg, Missouri; and Franklin Pierce in Concord, New Hampshire. The author believes that the memorials of these Presidents should have been located at the grave-site.

The pilgrimage to the graves of the Presidents began in 1929. While the graves have been visited and revisited on many occasions, it was necessary, in the interests of accuracy, to have the inscriptions verified by communicating with the persons in charge. The destructive action of age and the ravages of weather made many of the inscriptions difficult to read. In general, the response to the requests for information was prompt and cordial.

The following deserve commendation:

Mrs. M. W. Beasley, The Hollywood Cemetery, Richmond, Virginia (James Monroe, John Tyler, Jefferson Davis).

Joseph H. Schantz, The Village Cemetery, Kinderhook, New York (Martin Van Buren).

Mrs. Helen M. Sims, Forest Lawn Cemetery, Buffalo, New York (Millard Fillmore).

Oak Ridge Cemetery, Springfield, Illinois (Abraham Lincoln).

Lake View Cemetery, Cleveland, Ohio (James A. Garfield).

Albany Rural Cemetery, Menands, New York (Chester A. Arthur).

Crown Hill Cemetery, Indianapolis, Indiana (Benjamin Harrison).

James M. Callaghan, Youngs Memorial Cemetery, Oyster Bay, Long Island (Theodore Roosevelt).

J. Metzler, Arlington National Cemetery, Arlington, Virginia (William H. Taft, John F. Kennedy).

Al Johnson, The Congressional Cemetery, Washington, D. C. (Cenotaph of John Quincy Adams, temporary graves of William Henry Harrison, and Zachary Taylor).

Lewis B. Baughman, Zachary Taylor National Cemetery, Springfield, Kentucky (Zachary Taylor).

Clair B. Heyer, Hoover Presidential Library and Museum, West Branch, Iowa (Herbert Hoover).

John E. Wickman, Dwight D. Eisenhower Library, Abilene, Kansas (Dwight D. Eisenhower).

Mrs. Elizabeth R. Martin, Ohio Historical Society (McKinley).

John A. Matsko, The Lake View Cemetery Association (Garfield).

Mrs. Harold Augenstein, Harding Home and Museum, Marion, Ohio (Warren G. Harding).

Mrs. Mary Lewis, Executive Secretary, Nashville Rotary Club, and Sam B. Smith, Chairman. Tennessee Historical Commission (James K. Polk).

William Churchill Edwards, City Historian, Quincy, Massachusetts (The Adams Temple-Memorial to the second and sixth Presidents, John Adams and John Quincy Adams).

Mrs. Edna H. Miller and the Lancaster Pilot International Club, Lancaster, Pennsylvania (James Buchanan).

It is disappointing to record that, of the thirteen graves of the Presidents who were Masons (Washington, Monroe, Jackson, Polk, Buchanan, Andrew Johnson, Garfield, McKinley, Theodore Roosevelt, Taft, Harding, F. D. Roosevelt), only one of the graves has been marked by the Masonic Fraternity, that of Warren G. Harding.

Of the Presidents who have been credited to have been members of the Militia or the National Guard, no grave recognition has been placed on any grave by the National Guard Association:

President	State Guard
Washington	Virginia
Monroe	Virginia
Jackson	Tennessee
Tyler	Virginia
Atchison	Missouri
Pierce	New Hampshire
Buchanan	Pennsylvania
Jefferson Davis	Mississippi
Lincoln	Illinois
Grant	Illinois
Hayes	Ohio
Garfield	Ohio
Arthur	New York
Benjamin Harrison	Indiana
McKinley	Ohio
Theodore Roosevelt	New York

Gratitude is expressed to Robert H. Land of the Library of Congress for supplying a list of the works devoted exclusively to the graves of the Presidents.

I am profoundly grateful for the prompt response of Mr. Hibbard G. James of the Washington Cathedral, Mount Saint Alban, Washington, D.C., who provided the pictures of the tomb of Woodrow Wilson.

Thanks are due Mr. Charles P. Taft, son of President Taft, who supplied information concerning the designer of the Taft Monument in Arlington National Cemetery.

A word of appreciation is due Hoyer's Photo Supply of Williamsport, Pa., for copy reductions of the pictures used in this book.

I am profoundly indebted to Mrs. Pauline Clinton, librarian of the Green Free Library of Wellsboro, and to J. Russell Rowe, a member of the library staff, for their cheerful cooperation in searching for books now out of print or classified as "rare" books which I consulted as references.

For moral support, I am indebted not only to my wife, Ruth Washburn Laird, but also to my children Winthrop Washburn, Robert Hyslop, Elizabeth Louise, and Archibald Laird II, who, without a voice of dissent, cheerfully accompanied me, singly, or, as a group, on my Presidential Pilgrimage.

CONTENTS

ILLUSTRATIONS

INTRODUCTION

The monuments marking the burial places of the Presidents of the United States vary from simplicity to grandeur. They do not reflect the origin, the struggles, the achievements, nor the failures of the leaders of the greatest nation on earth.

Some graves are preserved in beauty and appropriateness, while others are neglected and forgotten. Cemeteries, which should be proud of their role as guardians of the remains of the Presidents committed to their care, are indifferent to that precious heritage.

Every President has made a valuable contribution to the nation. Those without station or formal education served with pride and faithfulness, and assumed their places alongside of those with a background of wealth, university training, and high social position. The common goal was service to the country.

A journey to their last resting places is a real and enduring inspiration, whether the mecca be a pantheon or a grassy mound.

This collection of pictures is designed to develop a sense of history in everyone who sees them. They may be the means of initiating an interesting pilgrimage, the memory of which will live forever.

The "grave" monuments represent men who guided the destiny of the United States in peace and war, in periods of domestic unrest, in tranquillity, in periods of affluence and in periods of economic depression.

There is no better way to keep alive their wisdom, patriotism, faith, determination, and genius than to look at their graves, thus being urged to renew allegiance to our country and pledge continuance of the lofty ideals they struggled to preserve.

GEORGE WASHINGTON

PRESIDENT OF
SIXTEEN STATES

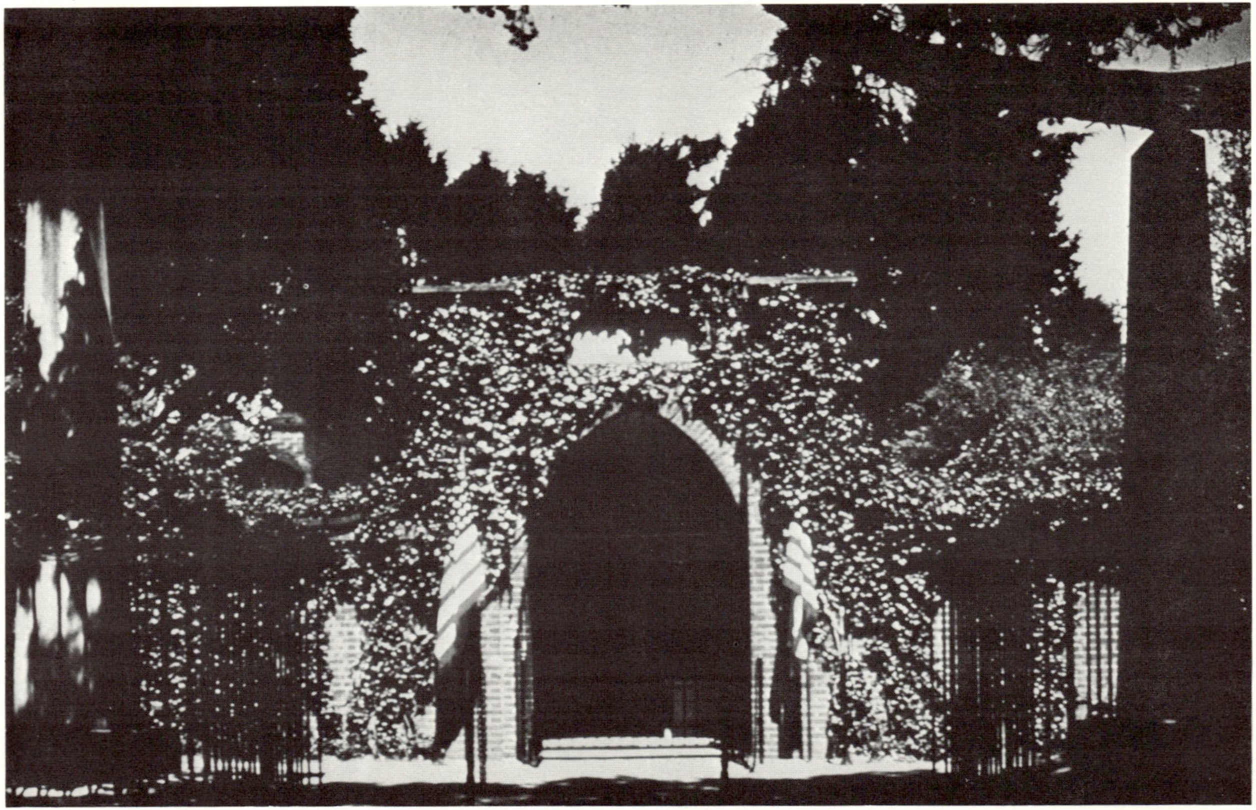

Tomb of George Washington

GEORGE WASHINGTON
1789–1797

The monument marking the grave of George Washington, the first President of the United States, is located at Mount Vernon, Virginia.

The tomb consists of a red brick mausoleum facing the Potomac River. The entrance to the mausoleum is a six-foot-wide, high arched aperture guarded by two eight-foot-high gates made of iron rods.

Above the apex of the entrance arch is a stone tablet which reads:

Within this Enclosure

rest

the remains of

Genl George Washington

Inside the mausoleum are the sarcophagi. The one on the right, as one faces the structure, and immediately behind the right gate, is the sarcophagus of George Washington. The top is ornamented by a sculptured replica of the coat of arms of the Washingtons. The base of the shield is inscribed:

WASHINGTON

A ridge along the midportion of the near end of the sarcophagus is inscribed:

George Washington

To the left of the left gate guarding the mausoleum and behind the front wall on the left as one faces the structure, is the plain sarcophagus of Martha Washington. The top of the sarcophagus carries the following:

Martha, Consort of Washington

On the near end, toward the front of the mausoleum, the inscription reads:

Died May 22, 1802
Age 70 Yr.

In the center of the wall behind the sarcophagi and approximately five feet above the tops of the sarcophagi is a marble slab carrying the quotation from St. John XI, 25, 26:

I am the resurrection, and
the life; he that believeth in me,
though he were dead, yet he shall
live: And whosoever liveth and believeth
in me SHALL NOT DIE.

Midway below the above plaque and the floor of the mausoleum is a perforated metal door which leads into the rear vault which contains the remains of about thirty members of the General's deceased relatives.

To permit easy access to this entrance to the rear vault, the sarcophagus of Martha Washington is located behind the left front wall of the mausoleum and is not in direct view as one faces the structure.

JOHN ADAMS

PRESIDENT OF
SIXTEEN STATES

Sarcophagus of John Adams

JOHN ADAMS
1797–1801

The Adams Monument

The monument marking the last resting place of John Adams, the second President of the United States and that of John Quincy Adams, the sixth President of the United States, is the First Parish Church (Unitarian) located in Quincy, Massachusetts.

Four generations of their ancestors were associated with the church prior to the birth of John Adams in 1735. In that year, the church organization was ninety-nine years old.

The first meeting house was dedicated in 1637, the second in 1666, the third in 1732, and the present church building, known as the Adams Temple, was dedicated in 1828.

The granite used in the construction of the sanctuary, with its domed ceiling, was a gift of President John Adams before he died on July 4, 1826. He had established the Adams Temple Fund in 1822. His remains, together with those of his wife, Abigail, were placed in the Crypt of the Temple on April 1, 1828.

The fourteen by fourteen foot space for the Crypt beneath the portico for these tombs was conveyed to John Quincy Adams for that purpose in 1827.

The portico is supported by four monoliths twenty-five feet high and weighing twenty-five tons each. The Doric monoliths were erected in June, 1828.

On September 1, 1852, the Church conveyed a space fourteen feet by fourteen feet adjoining that of John Adams and Abigail Adams to Charles Francis Adams upon which to erect tombs for his father, John Quincy Adams, and his mother, Louisa Catherine Adams. Their remains were transferred to the Crypt from the Hancock Cemetery on December 10, 1852.

The entire edifice is truly a monument to the second and sixth Presidents of the United States.

The spacious auditorium contains the Adams memorial plaques, and the pew of John Quincy Adams. The lower level contains the Crypts where the sarcophagi of John Adams and John Quincy Adams are located.

Courtesy of United First Parish Church

Top: Church of the Presidents: United First Parish Church
(Unitarian), Quincy, Massachusetts
Bottom: John Adams Plaque in Sanctuary

The following plaque is located on the wall of the Sanctuary:

John Adams
Libertatem, Amicitiam, Fidem, Retineris
D.O.M.
Beneath these walls
Are deposited the remains of

JOHN ADAMS

Son of John and Susanna (Boylston) Adams
Second President of the United States
Born 30 October 1735
On the Fourth of July 1776
He pledged his Life, Fortune and Sacred Honor
To the Independence of His Country
On the third of September 1783
He affixed his seal to the definitive Treaty with Great Britain
Which acknowledged that Independence,
And consummated the Redemption of his Pledge.
On the Fourth of July 1826
He was summoned
To the Independence of Immortality
And to the JUDGMENT OF HIS GOD
This House will bear witness to his Piety,
This town, his Birth-Place, to his Munificience,
History to his Patriotism,
Posterity to the Depth and Compass of his mind.
At his side
Sleeps till the Trumpet shall sound

ABIGAIL

His beloved and only wife
Daughter of William and Elizabeth (Quincy) Smith.
In every relation of Life a Pattern
Of Filial, Conjugal, Maternal and Social Virtue
Born November 8, 1744
Deceased 18 October 1818
Aged 74

Married 25 October 1764
During a Union of more than half a Century
They survived in Harmony of Sentiment, Principle, and Affection
The Tempests of Civil Commotion.
Meeting undaunted and Surmounting
The Terrors and Trials of that Revolution
Which secured the Freedom of their Country,
Improved the Condition of their Times
And brightened the Prospects of Futurity
To the Race of Man upon Earth.

PILGRIM

From lives thus spent, Thy earthly duties learn:
From Fancy's Dream to active Virtue turn;
Let Freedom, Friendship, Faith, thy soul engage,
And serve, like them, thy Country and thy Age.

The following plaques are located at the entrance to the Crypt of John Adams:

JOHN ADAMS

Signer of the Declaration of Independence
Framer of the Constitution of Massachusetts
Second President of the United States 1735–1826
The John Adams Chapter DAR caused this tablet to be affixed
1900

ABIGAIL ADAMS

As daughter, wife and mother
A Model of Domestic Worth
Her Letters are an American Classic
1744–1818
The Abigail Adams Chapter DAR caused this tablet to be affixed
1900

Tablets at Entrance to John Adams Crypt

THOMAS JEFFERSON

PRESIDENT OF
SEVENTEEN STATES

Thomas Jefferson Obelisk

THOMAS JEFFERSON
1801–1809

A rectangular plot of ground surrounded by an iron fence contains the grave of Thomas Jefferson, the third President of the United States. It is located at Monticello, Virginia.

A monument, a granite shaft, contains these words as directed by the will* of the Sage of Monticello:

Here was buried

Thomas Jefferson

Author of the Declaration of Independence

Of the Statute of Virginia for Religious Freedom

And the Father of the University of Virginia

Born April 13, 1743   Died July 4, 1826

*The obelisk to be six feet in height, and to carry the above inscription and "not one word more."

Two flat slabs, step like in construction, support the square base on which the obelisk stands.

In the Francis Quadrangle beside the entrance to Jesse Hall of the University of Missouri, Columbia, Missouri, is located the original tombstone of Thomas Jefferson. The base of the limestone obelisk contains all that remains of the original inscription:

Born April 2nd

1743, O S

Died July 4th 1826

Wind and rain have entirely obliterated the inscription on the shaft.

A bronze plaque affixed to the base of the obelisk facing the Quadrangle carries this message:

This Original Marker
Placed at the grave of Thomas Jefferson at Monticello
Virginia, in 1826. Constructed from his own design.
Was presented July 4, 1883, by the Jefferson heirs to the
University of Missouri, first State University to be
Founded in the Louisiana Territory purchased from
France during President Jefferson's administration.
The obelisk, dedicated on this campus at commencement,
June 4th, 1885, commemorates Thomas Jefferson, Third
President of the United States, whose faith in the
future of Western America and whose confidence in the
People has shaped our national ideals; commemorates
the Author of the Declaration of Independence and
of the Virginia Statute for Religious freedom.
Founder of the University of Virginia, fosterer of
Public Education in the United States.

"The Original Epitaph"
Here was buried
Thomas Jefferson
Author
Of the Declaration of
American Independence
of
The Statute of Virginia
For Religious Freedom and
Father of the University
Of Virginia
Born April 2nd
1743 O S
Died July 4, 1826

Original Tombstone of Thomas Jefferson, University
of Missouri Campus

Jefferson's own handwritten epitaph for his wife is preserved
in the Library of Congress and reads as follows:

To The
Memory
of
Martha Jefferson
Daughter of John Wayles
Born Oct 17, 1748 O.S.
Intermarried with
Thomas Jefferson
Jan 1, 1772
Torn From Him By Death
Sep. 6, 1782
This Monument of his love
So Inscribed.

Other members of the Jefferson Family interred in the Monticello plot are:

Elder daughter:

Martha Jefferson Randolph, daughter of Thomas Jefferson and Martha Wayles. Born Sept. 27, 1772. Intermarried with Thos. Mann Randolph Feb. 23, 1790. Died at Edgehill Oct. 10, 1836.

Younger daughter:

Maria Jefferson Eppes, Daughter of Thomas Jefferson and Martha Wayles. Born Aug. 1, 1778. Intermarried with John Wayles Eppes Oct. 13, 1797. Died Apr. 17, 1804.

Son-in-law:

Gov. Thomas Mann Randolph, son of Thomas Mann Randolph of Tuckahoe and Anne Cary. Born May 17, 1768. Intermarried with Martha Jefferson Feb. 23, 1790. Died June 28, 1828.

JAMES MADISON

PRESIDENT OF
NINETEEN STATES

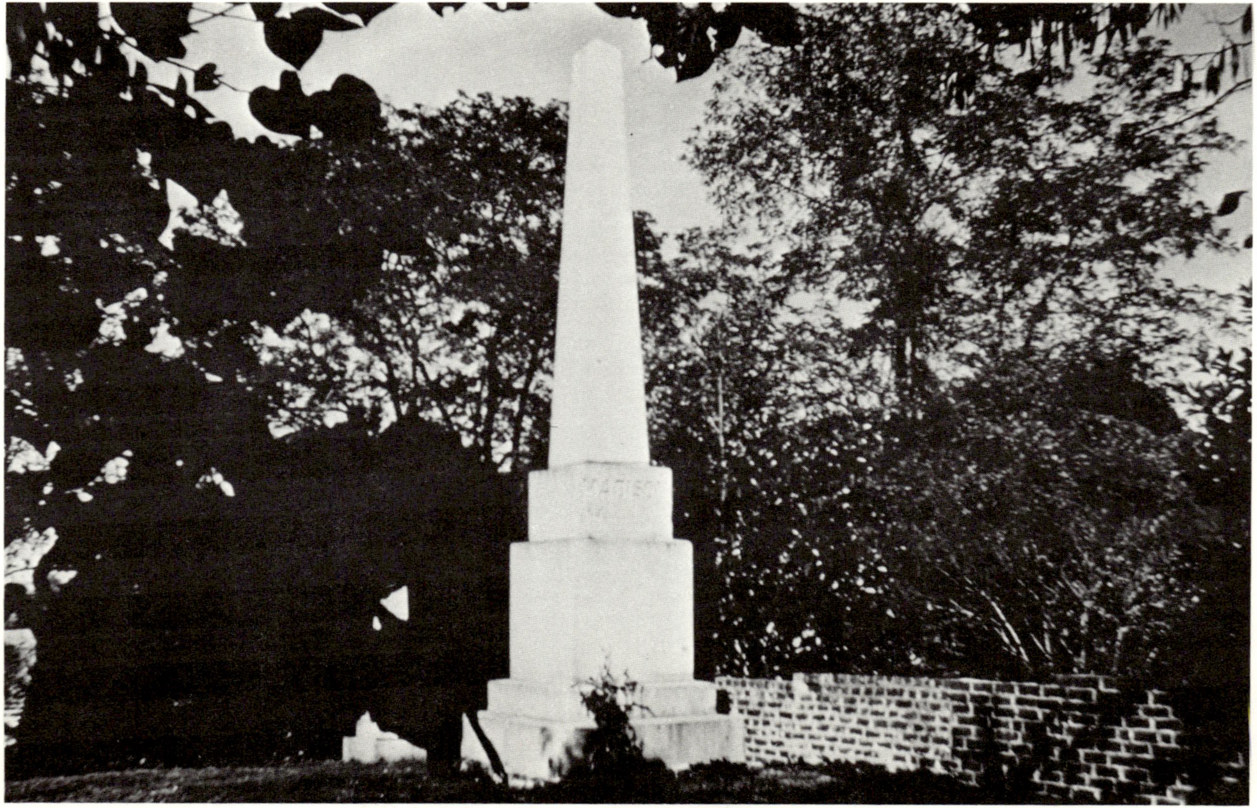

Grave of James Madison

JAMES MADISON
1809–1817

The monument marking the grave of James Madison, the fourth President of the United States is located in the Madison Cemetery on the grounds of his former home at Montpelier, Orange County, Virginia.

The entire cemetery is surrounded by a red brick wall three feet high. A bronze plaque is attached to the wall at the right of the cemetery entrance. The inscription reads:

1836   1936
In commemoration of the one hundredth
Anniversary of the death of
President James Madison
June 28, 1836
Erected by
The William Byrd Chapter of
Daughters of the American Revolution
Into whose charge this shrine
was given in 1950

The entire northern section of the cemetery, measuring twenty five feet by sixty-six feet, contains the graves of James Madison and his wife, Dolley Payne Madison.

A granite obelisk, ten feet in height, is supported by three square blocks of granite from six foot square at the turf level to two foot square at the base of the obelisk. The unadorned obelisk tapers from a two-foot square base to a one-foot square apex. The entire monument is twenty feet high. The east side bears the inscription.

Madison Obelisk

MADISON
BORN MARCH 16TH 1751
DIED JUNE 28TH 1836
J. W. Davies   Richd

William Byrd Chapter D.A.R. Tablet at Cemetery Entrance

Grave of Dolley Madison

Ten feet west, or in the rear of President Madison's monument, is a nine-foot high marble obelisk, fourteen inches square at the base and tapering to eight inches square at the summit, marking the grave of Mrs. Madison.

The shaft of the monument stands on a two-foot square marble base which in turn is supported by a granite base measuring two foot ten inches on each side.

The following inscription is located on the east side:

In
Memory
of
DOLLEY PAYNE
Wife of
JAMES MADISON
BORN
May 20, 1768
DIED
July 6, 1849
J. W. Davies
Richd

JAMES MONROE

PRESIDENT OF
TWENTY-FOUR STATES

Tomb of James Monroe

JAMES MONROE
1817–1825

The monument marking the grave of James Monroe, the fifth President of the United States, is located in the center of a circular plot forty-two feet in diameter. This plot is west of the burial plot of John Tyler in the Hollywood Cemetery, Richmond, Virginia. Nine feet, ten inches of the Monroe plot circumference forms the western border of the Tyler plot.

A twelve-foot long, six-foot wide, eighteen-foot high wrought iron structure resembling a cathedral covers the sarcophagus. The long axis of the tomb runs from east to west.

Brass plates, ten inches wide and twenty-two inches long are located on the east and west ends of the sarcophagus and are inscribed as follows:

James Monroe

Born in Westmoreland County

28' ' April 1758

Died in the City of New York

4' ' July 1831

By order of the General Assembly

His remains were removed

to this cemetery 5' ' July 1858

As an evidence of the affection of Virginia

For her good and honored son.

Near the northwest corner of the monument is a metal plate, flush with the turf, which is inscribed:

President

James Monroe

Revolutionary Soldier

1775–1778

Placed by

The Virginia Society, DAR

1953

Farther to the left as one faces the monument is a metal shield which states:

Maria Hester
Monroe
Gouverneur
Daughter of
President Monroe
Revolutionary
Soldier
Placed by
The Virginia
Society
DAR
1953

On the south, at the monument's west end, is a shield shaped metal plate flush with the turf which is inscribed:

Elizabeth
Kortright
Monroe
wife of
President James
Monroe
Placed by
The Virginia Society
DAR
1955

Beside the above shield is a rectangular metal plate inscribed:

Elizabeth Kortright Monroe
Wife of
President James Monroe
Born 1768 — Died September 23, 1830

Near the southwest corner is a circular metal plate enclosing a five pointed star. The circular portion states: In Honor of Service in the War of 1812. Within the star are:

N S

U S D

Another flush metal plate northwest of the monument is inscribed:

Maria Hestor Monroe Gouverneur
Daughter of
President James Monroe
Wife of
Samuel Lawrence Gouverneur
Born 1804 — Died June 20, 1850

The bodies of Mrs. James Monroe and Mrs. Gouverneur were removed from their Oak Hill resting place, home of President Monroe, and interred in the Monroe plot in the Hollywood Cemetery in 1903.

James Monroe died in a house located on Prince Street, New York City. A bronze tablet on the front of the house carried the following inscription:

In this house died
JAMES MONROE
Fifth President of the United States
Who Proclaimed
The Monroe Doctrine
Upon which depends
Freedom of American Republics and
The safety of the United States
Against Foreign Aggression
Born April 28, 1758, Died July 4, 1831
Soldier in the Continental Army
Member of the Continental Congress
American Envoy to Great Britain
France and Spain

Negotiator of the Louisiana Purchase
Secretary of State
Secretary of War
Twice Governor of Virginia
Twice President of the United States

Monroe's remains were removed from the Green—Wood Cemetery near Fort Hamilton, New York and interred in the Hollywood Cemetery, Richmond, Virginia, July 5, 1858.

The house, owned by Monroe's son-in-law, located near the corner of Prince Street and Lafayette Avenue, was torn down in 1929. The bronze memorial tablet vanished in 1967.

A resolution passed by the Virginia General Assembly on April 6, 1858 directed Governor Wise of Virginia to effect the removal of the remains of James Monroe from New York City to the Hollywood Cemetery, Richmond, Virginia and to erect a monument over the grave in the President's memory.

The architect of the monument was Albert Lybrock, a native of Alsace Lorraine. The firm making the ironwork covering the sarcophagus was Wood and Perrott of Philadelphia. The framework resembles a Norman Abbey.

JOHN QUINCY ADAMS

PRESIDENT OF
TWENTY-FOUR STATES

Tombs of John Quincy Adams and Louisa Catherine Adams

JOHN QUINCY ADAMS
1825–1829

John Quincy Adams
Alteri Seculo
Near this place
Reposes all that could die of
JOHN QUINCY ADAMS
Son of John and Abigail (Smith) Adams
Sixth President of the United States
Born 11 July, 1767
Amidst the Storms of Civil Commotion
He nursed the Vigor
Which nerves a Statesman and a Patriot
And the Faith
Which inspires a Christian.
For more than half a century,
Whenever his Country called for his labors
In either Hemisphere or in any capacity
He never spared them in her cause.
On the 24 of December, 1814
He signed the Second Treaty with Great Britain
Which restored peace within her borders.
On the 23 of February 1848
He closed sixteen years of
Eloquent Defense of the lessons of his youth
By dying at his Post
In her great National Council
A son worthy of his father.
A citizen, shedding glory on his country
A Scholar, ambitious to advance Mankind
This Christian sought to walk humbly
In the sight of his God.

Beside him lies
His partner for fifty years
LOUISA CATHERINE
Daughter of Joshua and Catherine (Nuth) Johnson
Born, 12 February, 1775
Married 26 July, 1797
Deceased, 15 May, 1852
Age 77
"Living through many Vicissitudes, and
Under High Responsibilities
As a daughter, wife and mother
She proved equal to all
Dying, she left to her family and her sex
the blessed remembrance
Of a woman that feareth the Lord"

"Herein is that saying true: One soweth and another reapeth. I left you reap that whereon ye bestowed no labor. Other men labored, and ye are entered into their labors."

At the entrance to the crypt of John Quincy Adams the following plaques are found:

LOUISA CATHERINE ADAMS
Frail of Body, Simple in Tastes, and retiring in Nature,
She filled the onerous positions to which it pleased God
To assign her, with grace, dignity and fortitude
1775–1852
The Abigail Phillips Quincy Chapter DAR caused this tablet
to be affixed 1930

JOHN QUINCY ADAMS

Diplomat, Senator, Congressman, Secretary of State
Negotiator of Peace Treaty with England 1814
Sixth President of the United States
1767–1848

The Abigail Phillips Quincy Chapter DAR caused this tablet
to be affixed 1927

Plaques at Entrance to John Quincy Adams Crypt

The body of John Quincy Adams was temporarily interred in the Congressional Cemetery, Washington, D.C., following his death in the House of Representatives February 23, 1848. The John Quincy Adams Cenotaph is located in the Congressional Cemetery.

The inscription on the Congressional Cemetery Cenotaph reads:

The Honorable
JOHN QUINCY ADAMS
A Representative
in the
Congress of the
United States from
THE STATE OF
MASSACHUSETTS
Died Feb. 23, 1848
Age 79 Years

Left: John Quincy Adams Plaque in Sanctuary
Right: John Quincy Adams Cenotaph in Congressional Cemetery

ANDREW JACKSON

PRESIDENT OF
TWENTY-SIX STATES

Grave of Andrew Jackson

ANDREW JACKSON
1829–1837

President Jackson's grave is located on the grounds of the Hermitage, near Nashville, Tennessee.

The grave monument is a modified Greek peristyle temple with eight columns supporting a high domed copper cupola.

His inscription reads:

General
Andrew Jackson
Born on the 15th of March, 1767
Died on the 8th of June, 1845

The inscription on the tomb of his wife, who rests by his side, reads:

"Here lies the remains of Mrs. Rachel Jackson, wife of President Jackson, who died the 22 of December, 1828, aged 61 years. Her face was fair, her person pleasing, her temper amiable, her heart kind; she delighted in relieving the wants of her fellow creatures, and cultivated that divine pleasure by the most liberal and unpretending methods; to the poor, she was a benefactor; to the rich, an example; to the wretched, a comforter; to the prosperous, an ornament; her piety went hand in hand with her benevolence, and she thanked her creator for being permitted to do good. A being so gentle and so virtuous, slanders might wound, but could not dishonor; even death, when he bore her from the arms of her husband, could but transport her to the bosom of God."

These inscriptions are found on the base supporting a small pyramid shaped shaft of marble located in the center of the cupola.

MARTIN VAN BUREN

PRESIDENT OF
TWENTY-SIX STATES

Obelisk of Martin Van Buren

MARTIN VAN BUREN
1837–1841

The monument marking the grave of Martin Van Buren, the eighth President of the United States, is located in the Village Cemetery, Kinderhook, New York.

It consists of a tall, unadorned grey granite obelisk, whose base measures thirty-four inches by thirty-four inches and is twenty-three and one-fourth inches high. The shaft measures twenty-five and one half inches by twenty-five and one half inches at the base and tapers to one foot by one foot at the summit. The shaft from its base to the summit is twelve feet high.

The entire monument is supported by a four foot by four foot base, fifteen inches high.

The west side of the obelisk is inscribed:

MARTIN VAN BUREN
VIIIth PRESIDENT
OF THE UNITED STATES
BORN DEC. 5, 1782
DIED JULY 24, 1862

—

HANNAH VAN BUREN
His Wife
Born Mar. 8, 1783
Died at Albany, N.Y.
Feb. 5, 1819

(Her body was moved to the Kinderhook Cemetery in 1855)

The south side of the shaft is inscribed:
Martin son of Martin
and Hannah Van Buren
Born Dec 30, 1812
Died at Paris, France
Mar. 19, 1855

Headstones fourteen inches high and one foot wide at the base of the monument are lettered:

MVB   HVB   MVB, Jr.

Directly behind the obelisk, East, are four flat white marble slabs inscribed as follows:

Slab #1

She was a sincere Christian
dutiful child, tender mother
and most affectionate wife,
Precious shall be the memory of her virtues

Slab #2

Sacred
To the memory of
Mrs. Hannah Van Buren
Wife of
Martin Van Buren
who departed this life
on the 5th of February
AD 1819 in the 36th
year of her
age

Slab #3

Beneath this tomb
rests the remains of
the first person intered
in this cemetery
Removed to this place
from Albany in 1855

Slab #4

Blessed are the dead which
die in the Lord from henceforth; Yea saith the Spirit,
that they may rest from
their labours; and their
works do follow them.

Darling, Sculpt.

Hudson

WILLIAM HENRY HARRISON

PRESIDENT OF
TWENTY-SIX STATES

Tower Marking Grave of William Henry Harrison

WILLIAM HENRY HARRISON
March 4–April 4, 1841

William Henry Harrison, the ninth President is buried in the Harrison Memorial Park (formerly known as the Congress Green Cemetery) at North Bend, Ohio.

His grave is marked by a seventy-five-foot high sandstone tower, erected in 1921.

W. H. Harrison was born at Berkeley, Charles City County, Virginia, February 9, 1773. He was graduated from the Hampden-Sidney College and entered upon the study of medicine at the University of Pennsylvania. He withdrew from the medical school and elected to enter the United States Army in 1791.

Governor of the Northwest Territory 1801
Hero of Tippicanoe 1811
Representative in Congress 1816–1819
Ohio Legislature 1824
U.S. Senate 1825 (Resigned)
Minister to Columbia 1828
Elected President 1840
Inaugurated President March 4, 1841
Died April 3, 1841 at the age of 68

His initial burial place was in the Congressional Cemetery, Washington, D.C.

JOHN TYLER

PRESIDENT OF
TWENTY-SEVEN STATES

Grave Monument of John Tyler

JOHN TYLER
1841–1845

The monument marking the grave of John Tyler, the tenth President of the United States, is located in a plot which measures twenty-seven feet, eight inches along the Presidents' Circle Road in the Hollywood Cemetery, Richmond, Virginia. The north and south borders of the plot extend westward thirty-two feet, inclining toward each other until they reach the circumference of the President James Monroe plot. At this point the measurement is nine feet ten inches.

A monolithic granite shaft occupies the front and northern portion of the Tyler plot. The shaft is twenty-five feet high and is crowned by a bronze Greek urn supported by two American eagles. An heroic bust, in bronze, of the President, facing east, rests on a pedestal. Beneath the bust is this inscription:

JOHN TYLER
PRESIDENT
OF THE
UNITED STATES
1841–1845
Born
In Charles City County
March 29, 1790
Died
In the City of Richmond
January 18, 1862

On the north side of the monolith is a bas-relief of a male figure bearing a shield containing the seals of the United States and the state of Virginia in the left hand, significant of his relations with the National Government and his native state. The hand of the extended right arm holds faggots.

The bas-relief on the south side carries a draped female figure representing memory. She holds a laurel wreath in the left hand. The right hand is symbolically cultivating the young tree of the Republic, which, during Tyler's administration, began to grow and expand in an exceptional manner.

Beneath the bas-relief on the north face of the paneled monolith is this inscription:

Erected by the Congress of the United States
MCMXV

A flag holder in front of the President Tyler monument states:

In Honor of Service
In the War of 1812
John Tyler

Members of the Tyler family buried in the President Tyler plot, in addition to President John Tyler and Julia Gardiner Tyler, are:

Julia Tyler
William Wallace
Anne B. Tyler
Lachlan Tyler
Robert L. Tyler
Henry Tyler
Lyon G. Tyler, Sr.
Mrs. Pearl Tyler Ellis

West of the President Tyler monument is a stone which records that:

Julia Tyler died 2nd
Monday in May 1871
Age 21
Of such is the Kingdom of Heaven

The inscription on the west side of the monument reads:
President John Tyler
Married first
Letitia Christian
Born November 12, 1790
Died September 10, 1842
Interred at Cedar Grove
New Kent County, Va.
Married Second
Julia Gardiner
Born July 23, 1820
Died July 10, 1889
Interred by his side
Under this monument.

The John Tyler monument was financed by an Act of Congress August 24, 1912. It was unveiled October 12, 1915.

JAMES KNOX POLK

PRESIDENT OF
THIRTY STATES

Tomb of James K. Polk

JAMES KNOX POLK
1845–1849

James Knox Polk, the eleventh President of the United States, is buried on the grounds of the State Capitol, Nashville, Tennessee. The superstructure covering the grave resembles a small Roman temple. The granite roof is supported by four Doric columns. The grave site of President and Mrs. Polk is located near the northeast corner of the Capitol grounds.
The frieze carries the following:
JAMES KNOX POLK
President of the U.S. Born Nov. 2, 1795 Died June 15, 1849

The granite block over the grave is inscribed on the east:
The Mortal Remains of
JAMES KNOX POLK
Are resting in the vault beneath
He was born in MecKlenburg County
North Carolina
And migrated with his father
Samuel Polk to Tennessee
In 1806
The Beauty of Virtue
Was illustrated in his life
The excellence of Christianity
Was exemplified in his death

———

SARAH CHILDRESS
WIFE OF JAMES KNOX POLK
1803   1891

On the north the inscription reads:

By his public policy he defined, established and extended the boundaries of his Country. He planted the laws of the American Union on the shores of the PACIFIC. His influence and his Counsels united to organize the National Treasury on the principles of the Constitution, and to apply the rule of Freedom to Navigation, Trade and Industry.

On the south the inscription reads:

His life was devoted to the public service. He was elevated successively to the first places in the State and Federal Governments. A member of the General Assembly, a member of Congress and Chairman of the most important Congressional Committees: Speaker of the House of Representatives, Governor of Tennessee and President of the United States.

On the west the inscription reads:

"Asleep in Jesus."
SARAH CHILDRESS POLK,
wife of
JAMES KNOX POLK
Born in Rutherford County, Tenn.,
Sept. 4, 1803,
Died at Polk Place, Nashville, Tenn.,
August 14, 1891

A noble woman, a devoted wife, a true
friend, a sincere Christian.

"Blessed are the dead
which die in the Lord"

DAVID RICE ATCHISON

PRESIDENT OF
THIRTY STATES

Atchison Cemetery Plot Monument

DAVID RICE ATCHISON
March 4, 1849

David Rice Atchison, President of the United States for a day, is buried in the Greenlawn Cemetery, Plattsburg, Missouri.
Born August 11, 1807
Died January 26, 1886
A plain headstone marks his grave.

A statue was erected to his memory in Plattsburg by an act of the Missouri 54th General Assembly, and unveiled in front of the Clinton County Court House on October 27, 1928. The plaque on the base of the statue reads:
DAVID RICE ATCHISON
1807–1886
President of the United States
One Day
Lawyer, Statesman & Jurist
U.S. Senate 1843–1855
Erected by the State of Missouri

Left: Statue of David Rice Atchison
Right: David Rice Atchison Headstone

MALCOLM ZACHARY TAYLOR

PRESIDENT OF
THIRTY STATES

Statue and Mausoleum of Zachary Taylor

ZACHARY TAYLOR
March 5, 1849–July 9, 1850

Zachary Taylor is buried in a granite mausoleum located in the Zachary Taylor National Cemetery (formerly the Taylor family burying ground) in Springfield, Kentucky. His name appears over the entrance to the mausoleum.

Nearby is a thirty-four-foot high granite shaft supporting a marble statue of General Taylor. The base of the monument contains four shields. The shield in the front bears the following inscription:

Major General Zachary Taylor
12th President of the United States
Born Nov. 24, 1784
Died July 9, 1850

Above this shield are the superimposed letters — (Z T)

The left shield (moving clockwise around the monument) carries:

Palo Alto
Resaca De La Palma
Monterrey
Beuna Vista

The rear shield:

U S Insignia with 13 stars.

The right shield:

Fort Harrison
Black Hawk
Okeechobee

In the space above the ZT monogram is this quotation:

"I have endevored to do my duty, I am ready to die, my only regret is for the friends I leave behind me"

Midway between this inscription and the base of the statue on top is a metal disc bearing the likeness of the face of General Taylor.

MILLARD FILLMORE

PRESIDENT OF
THIRTY-ONE STATES

Grave of Millard Fillmore

MILLARD FILLMORE
July 9, 1850–March 4, 1853

The monument marking the grave of Millard Fillmore, thirteenth President of the United States, is located in the Forest Lawn Cemetery, Buffalo, New York. The Fillmore plot is surrounded by an iron fence. In the center of the plot is a shaft of Scotch pink granite on which the following is inscribed:

On the front of the monument:

MILLARD FILLMORE

Born

January 7, 1800

Died

March 8, 1874

On the base:

FILLMORE

On the right side:

Abigail Powers

Fillmore

Wife of

Millard Fillmore

Born March 13, 1798

Died March 30, 1853

On the rear of the monument:

Millard Powers Fillmore

Born

April 25, 1828

Died November 15, 1889

Mary Abigail Fillmore

Born

March 27, 1832

Died July 26, 1854

On the left side:

Caroline Carmichael
Wife of
Millard Fillmore
Born Oct. 21, 1813
Died Aug. 11, 1881

A bronze plaque on the metal fence enclosure reads:
In Memory
of
MILLARD FILLMORE
13th President of the
United States of America
Born January 7, 1800   Died March 8, 1874
Dedicated by the Millard Fillmore Republican Woman's Club
Memorial Day May 30, 1932
A simple granite memorial marker bears the letters "M F"
indicating the grave of President Fillmore.

FRANKLIN PIERCE

PRESIDENT OF
THIRTY-ONE STATES

Grave of Franklin Pierce

FRANKLIN PIERCE
1853–1857

The second monument marking the grave of Franklin Pierce was authorized and erected by the Legislature of New Hampshire in 1947. It stands in the Minot Cemetery, Concord, New Hampshire. It consists of a granite base supporting a tapered, fluted column which is crowned by a trefoil cross. The horizontal arms of the cross support a draped robe, symbolic of his laying aside the mantle of leadership.

In the shallow of the recess in the base of the monument is inscribed:

FRANKLIN PIERCE
BORN NOV. 23, 1804
DIED OCT. 8, 1869
14TH PRESIDENT
OF THE
UNITED STATES
1853–1857
P I E R C E

On a slab attached at the left of the base of the monument is inscribed:

JANE M. APPLETON
Wife Of
Franklin Pierce
Born Mar. 12, 1806
Died Dec. 2, 1863

The slab attached to the right of the Pierce monument reads:

Their Children
Frank R. Pierce
Born Aug. 27, 1839
Died Nov. 14, 1843

Benjamin Pierce
Born Apr. 13, 1841
Died Jan. 6, 1853

The State of New Hampshire erected a statue in honor of Franklin Pierce on the State House grounds in 1914. The Inscription on the East Side reads:

Franklin Pierce
Fourteenth
President
Of The
United States

On the North Side:

Born at Hillsborough, New Hampshire
Nov. 23, 1804
A lawyer who loved his profession
And was a great leader in it.
Member of the New Hampshire Legislature
At 25, and speaker at 27
Congressman at 29
United States Senator at 32, and
Resigned at 37
Later in life, declined the office
Of Attorney General of the United
States, That of Secretary of War,
The United States Senatorship, and
Governor of his State

———

President of the New Hampshire
Constitutional Convention;
President of the United States
Died at Concord, Oct. 8, 1869

Franklin Pierce Statue

On the South Side:

Brigadier General of the U.S.A.
Puebla
Contreras
Cherumbusco
Monteno Del Rey
Chapultepec
Commissioner appointed by
General Scott to arrange an Armistice
With General Santa Anna.
"He was a gentleman and a man of
Courage." Ulysses S. Grant

On the West Side;

Erected by the
State of New Hampshire
1914

Franklin Pierce Historical Marker

FRANKLIN PIERCE
(1804–1869)
Fourteenth President of the United States
(1853–1857)
Lies buried in nearby Minot enclosure.
Native son of New Hampshire,
graduate of Bowdoin College,
lawyer, effective political leader,
Congressman and U.S. Senator,
Mexican War veteran, courageous
advocate of States' Rights,
he was popularly known as
"Young Hickory of the Granite Hills."

State of New Hampshire Historical Marker near the cemetery.

JAMES BUCHANAN

PRESIDENT OF
THIRTY-FOUR STATES

Grave of James Buchanan

JAMES BUCHANAN
1857–1861

The second monument marking the grave of President James Buchanan was erected by the Lancaster Chapter of the Pilot Club International in 1960. The memorial is of Barre granite, and replaces the original of Italian marble which marked his grave in the Woodward Hill Cemetery, Lancaster, Pennsylvania.

The inscription reads:

Here rest the remains of
JAMES BUCHANAN
FIFTEENTH PRESIDENT OF THE UNITED STATES
BORN IN FRANKLIN COUNTY, PA., APRIL 23, 1791
DIED AT WHEATLAND, JUNE 1, 1868.

A flag holder in front of the monument reads:

In Honor of Service
In the War of 1812

In the center of a five pointed star which is surrounded by the above inscription are the initials:

N S
U S D

JEFFERSON DAVIS

PRESIDENT OF
THIRTEEN STATES

Jefferson Davis Circle, Hollywood Cemetery

JEFFERSON DAVIS
1861–1865

Jefferson Davis, who shared the leadership of thirteen states of the United States, is buried in the Hollywood Cemetery, Richmond, Virginia, not far from the graves of James Monroe and John Tyler.

An heroic statue of the Confederate President stands on a rectangular base, the front side of which bears the following inscription:

JEFFERSON DAVIS
At Rest
An American Soldier and Defender of the Constitution
Born in Kentucky 1808 and died in New Orleans, La. 1889
West Point 1828
House of Representatives Mississippi 1846–1847
Colonel Mississippi Rifles 1846–1847
Brigadier General USA 1847
Senator 1847–1851
Secretary of War 1853–1857
Senator 1857–1861

Inscription on rear of monument:
PRESIDENT CONFEDERATE STATES OF AMERICA
1861–1865
Faithful to all trusts, a martyr to principle
He lived and died the most consistent of American
Soldiers and Statesmen

North Side of Monument:
Sacred to the Memory of
Varina Howell Davis
Beloved & faithful wife of
Jefferson Davis

And devoted mother of his children
"Her children arise up & call her
Blessed: Her husband also and he
Praiseth her". "She stretcheth out her
hand to the poor; Yea she reacheth
forth her hands to the needy."
Give her of the fruit of her hands;
And let her own works praise her
in the gates

South side of the monument:
Erected By
Margaret Howell Davis Hayes,
The devoted daughter of
Jefferson & Varina Howell Davis
In the year of our Lord 1907.
"Whom God hath joined together
Let no man put asunder."
"Lord keep their memories green."

Blessed are they which are persecuted
for righteousness sake for theirs is
the Kingdom of Heaven.

Erected by his wife
Varina Howell Davis
and his daughter
Margaret Howell Davis Hayes
Nov. 9, 1899

The remains of Jefferson Davis were removed from the Metairie Cemetery, New Orleans, Louisiana and interred in the Hollywood Cemetery, Richmond, Virginia, May 31, 1893.

In front and on the left, a foot stone records:
Jefferson Davis
At Rest Deo Vindice
Born June 3, 1808
Died Dec. 6, 1889

Top: (left) Margaret Howell Davis Hayes Grave (right) Grave of
the Daughter of the Confederacy
Bottom: (left) Jefferson Davis Statue Over His Grave (right) Grave
of Jefferson Davis, Jr.

Flush with the turf in front of the foot stone, a bronze plaque carries this inscription:

In Memory of
Jefferson Davis
The first honorary member of
Kappa Sigma Fraternity
Dedicated by the Brothers of
Beta Beta Chapter of
Kappa Sigma Fraternity
April 29, 1966

In front of the monument and on the right, a foot stone records:

Varina Howell Davis
At Peace
Born May 7, 1826
Died Oct. 16, 1906

The heroic statue of Jefferson Davis stands on a pedestal in the center of a circle sixty-six feet in diameter. George Julian Zoinay was the sculptor. The statue was cast by the Henry-Bonnard Bronze, New York in 1899.

Both graves are covered with English Ivy.

To the west of the Jefferson Davis statue and within the inner circle is a monument to the eldest daughter of Jefferson Davis and Varina Howell Davis.

The monument depicts a woman facing east with her head bowed in grief, covered by a robe of mourning, supporting her arms on the pages of an upright open Bible.

On the base of the stone supporting the open Bible is this inscription:

"Oh Lord in thee I have trusted
Let me never be confounded"

On the granite slab covering the entire grave on the north and read from that direction is the following:

Margaret Howell Davis Hayes
Daughter of Jefferson & Varina Howell Davis
Died July 18, 1908

On the granite slab covering the entire grave on the left as one faces the open Bible, and read from the south, is this inscription:

Joel Addison Hayes
Born Holly Springs, Mississippi, Mar. 4, 1848
Died January 26, 1917

Across the foot of the slab, and read as one faces west, is the following:

Served with the
Confederate Army

A seated guardian angel, holding a wreath in her left hand, presents a restful tableau over the grave of the Daughter of the Confederacy, Varina Anne Davis. This monument faces the Jefferson Davis statue, to the south.

The south side of the monument carries this inscription:

VARINA ANNE DAVIS
DAUGHTER OF THE CONFEDERACY
The beloved child of
Jefferson Davis, President
of the Confederate States of America
and Varina Howell Davis

The East side:

Born in the Executive Mansion
Richmond, Virginia
Died Sept. 18, 1898*
at Narragansett Pier
Rhode Island

*A plaque in St. Paul's Episcopal Church, Richmond, records the date of birth as 27 July 1864.

The West side of the monument is inscribed:
> The whole country touched
> By her blameless and heroic career
> Mingled its tears with those
> Who knew and loved her.
> He giveth his beloved sleep.

The North side is inscribed:

ERECTED BY THE UNITED DAUGHTERS
OF THE CONFEDERACY, NOV. 9, 1899.

> In the flower of her beauty, rarely
> Gifted in intellect, this noble woman
> trustfully rendered up her stainless
> Soul to the God who gave it.
> Brave & steadfast, her loyal spirit
> Was worthy of her peoples'
> Glorious History.

North and east of the monument to the Daughter of the Confederacy is the grave of Jefferson Davis, Jr. This grave is marked by a broken column at the head of the grave and a foot stone at the opposite end. The area between these two markers is planted with English Ivy. The base of the column facing north carries the following inscription:
> Here rests
> Jefferson Davis, Jr.
> the last surviving & well
> beloved son of
> Jefferson and
> Varina Howell Davis

The west side of the base reads:
> He offered himself a willing
> sacrifice to duty and on the

threshold of an honorable and
useful manhood succumbed
to the pestilence he braved.

The south side reads:
He died respected, beloved
and mourned by his friends
and his fellow citizens.

The east side is inscribed:
"The Lord gave and the
Lord hath taken away.
Blessed be the name of the
Lord".

The foot stone on the south reads:
Sacred
to the memory of
Jefferson Davis, Jr.
Born Jan. 16, 1857
Died Oct. 16, 1878

Children and grandchildren of Jefferson Davis are buried
between the road of the Jefferson Davis Circle and the inner
sidewalk circle which encloses the three monuments to the Con-
federate President, his wife and two daughters:
Joseph Davis
Samuel Davis
Jefferson Davis, Jr.
Jefferson Davis Hayes
Jefferson Davis Hayes, Jr.
Elizabeth Davis Hayes
William Howell Davis

Lincoln Mausoleum Exterior

ABRAHAM LINCOLN

PRESIDENT OF
TWENTY-THREE STATES

Lincoln Mausoleum Interior

ABRAHAM LINCOLN
1861–1865

The monument marking the grave of Abraham Lincoln, the sixteenth President of the United States, is a mausoleum located in the Oak Ridge Cemetery, Springfield, Illinois.

Its seventy-two-foot square base, approximately sixteen feet high, has twenty-three-foot long elliptical projections on the north and south sides of the monument. Two flights of twenty-three steps, one on either side of the south projection, lead to the roof of the mausoleum in front, while two flights of twenty-four steps lead to the roof in the rear.

On the ground level, in front of the entrance to the mausoleum, is a bronze cast of the head of Lincoln, resting on a granite base. On the wall, just above the entrance to the ground floor of the mausoleum, is a bronze tablet containing the Gettysburg Address.

The superstructure on the roof of the mausoleum consists of four granite pedestals with an obelisk in the center thereof rising to the height of approximately one hundred eighteen feet. Beginning at the left front of the superstructure and moving in a counterclockwise direction, the pedestals support bronze group statues representing the Infantry, Cavalry, Artillery, and Navy, the branches of the Armed Forces under the Commander-In-Chief during the Civil War.

In front of the base of the obelisk is an heroic bronze statue of Lincoln holding the Emancipation Proclamation in his left hand. The bronze plaque on the base of the pedestal supporting the statue depicts an Eagle holding a broken chain in its beak.

Beneath the Eagle is the word LINCOLN.

Shields representing all states and territories of the United States form a ninety-six-foot symbolic chain around the pedestals and obelisk.

Designated a National Historic Landmark

Just beneath the shields of Florida and Tennessee is the
SERVIUS TULLIUS STONE that was sent to the United
States in 1865 by the citizens of Rome. The inscription of the
Stone in Latin reads:

Abrahamo Lincolnio
Region Folderat Americ Praesidi 11
HVNC EX Servi Tulli Aggere Lapidem
Ovo Vtrivsobe
Libertatis Adsertoris Fortiss
Memoria Conivncatvr
Cives Romani
D
A MDCCCLXV

To Abraham Lincoln President
For the second time of the American Republic, Citizens of Rome
Present this stone from the
Wall of Servius Tullius by
which the memory of each of
those brave advocates of Liberty may be associated.
Anno 1865

*   *   *

This Stone was received in
Washington, D.C. in 1865 and re-
mained there until 1870 when it
was transferred to the posses-
sion of the National Lincoln
Monument Association by joint
resolution of the Congress.

Twenty-five centuries after
being first placed by the
hands of man in the Ancient
walls of Rome, this stone was
dedicated as a part of the
Lincoln Tomb October 11, 1936
by Henry Horner, Governor of
Illinois

In the anterior rotunda of the mausoleum there is a replica of the Statue of Lincoln, the original of which is in the Lincoln Memorial, Washington, D.C.

Behind this statue, on the left, is a bronze plaque carrying a brief biography of Abraham Lincoln by H. A. Converse. On the same wall, to the right, is a bronze plaque which records Lincoln's Farewell Address to the Citizens of Springfield.

Plaque number three carries Lincoln's Gettysburg Address, and plaque number four contains his Second Inaugural Address.

In This Tomb Are The Remains Of
Abraham Lincoln
Sixteenth President Of The United States

Plaque #1

Born February 12, 1809, in a log cabin at Hodgenville, Kentucky, a slave state, second child of Thomas Lincoln and Nancy Hanks, died at Washington, D.C. April 15, 1865. Taken by his parents, in 1816, to Spencer County, Indiana, where he spent his youth. Two years later left motherless, but upon the remarriage of his father became strongly attached to his step-mother, Sarah Bush, who exerted great influence on his character. At the age of twenty-one came with his family overland to Macon County, Illinois, where they settled on a farm. In 1831 moved to New Salem, where he lived six years, moved to Springfield and practiced law until 1860, when he was elected to the Presidency of the United States. On November 4, 1842, married Mary Todd to which union were born four children, Robert Todd, Edward Baker, William Wallace and Thomas. Served as a captain in the Black Hawk War, four terms in the Illinois State Legislature, one term in Congress. Was twice defeated for the United States Senate, was twice elected President of the United States. With only a meager schooling he became a master of the English language, a nationally known orator and debater, and one of the world's greatest statesmen. He guided our nation through the Civil War and preserved our Union for posterity.

Plaque #2

FAREWELL ADDRESS

Friends, no one who has never been placed in a like position can understand my feelings at this hour, nor the oppressive sadness I feel at this parting.

For more than a quarter of a century I have lived among you, and during all that time I have received nothing but kindness at your hands. Here I have lived from my youth until now I am an old man. Here the most sacred ties of earth were assumed; here all my children were born; and one of them lies buried.

To you, dear friends, I owe all that I have, all that I am. All the strange checkered past seems to crowd now up on my mind. Today I leave you; I go to assume a task more difficult than that which devolved upon General Washington.

Unless the great God, who assisted him, shall be with and aid me, I must fail. But if the Omniscient Mind and the same Almighty Arm that directed and protected him, shall guide and support me, I shall not fail — I shall succeed. Let us all pray that the God of our fathers may not forsake us now. To Him I commend you all. Permit me to ask, that with equal sincerity and faith, you all will invoke His wisdom and guidance for me.

With these few words, I must leave you — for how long I know not, Friends, one and all, I must now bid you an affectionate farewell.

Springfield, Illinois
February 11, 1861

GETTYSBURG ADDRESS

Fourscore and seven years ago our fathers brought forth on this continent a new nation, conceived in liberty and dedicated to the proposition that all men are created equal. Now we are engaged in a great civil war, testing whether that nation, or any nation so conceived and so dedicated, can long endure. We are met on a great battlefield of that war. We have come to dedicate a portion of that field as a final resting place for those who here gave their lives that that nation might live. It is altogether fitting and proper that we do this, but, in a larger sense, we cannot dedicate — we cannot hallow — this ground. The brave men, living and dead, who struggled here, have consecrated it far above our poor power to add or detract. The world will little note or long remember what we say here, but it can never forget what they did here. It is for us, the living, rather, to be dedicated here to the unfinished work which they, who fought here, have thus far so nobly advanced. It is rather for us to be here dedicated to the great task remaining before us — that from these honored dead we take increased devotion to that cause for which they gave the last full measure of devotion, that we here highly resolve that these dead shall not have died in vain, that this nation, under God, shall have a new birth of freedom, and that government of the people, by the people, for the people, shall not perish from the earth.

Gettysburg, Pennsylvania
November 19, 1863

Courtesy of Oak Ridge Cemetery

Top: (left) Lincoln, "The Ranger" (right) Lincoln, "The Soldier"
Bottom: (left) Lincoln, "The Circuit Rider" (right) Lincoln, "The
Debater"

Plaque #4

SECOND INAUGURAL ADDRESS

"The Almighty has His own purposes, woe unto the world because of offenses! For it needs be that offenses come; but woe unto the man by whom offenses cometh. If we shall suppose that American slavery is one of those offenses which having continued through His appointed time, He now wills to remove, and that He gives both North and South this terrible war, as the woe due those by whom the offense came, shall we discern therein any departure from those divine attributes which believers in a living God always ascribe to Him? Fondly do we hope — fervently do we pray — that this mighty scourge of war may speedily pass away. Yet, if God wills that it continue until all the wealth piled by the bondsman's two hundred and fifty years of unrequited toil shall be sunk, and until every drop of blood drawn with the lash shall be paid by another drawn with the sword, as was said three thousand years ago, so still it must be said, the judgments of the Lord are true and righteous altogether.

With malice toward none, with charity for all; with firmness in the right, as God gives us to see the right, let us strive on to finish the work we are in; to bind up the nation's wounds; to care for him who shall have borne the battle, and for his widow, and his orphan — to do all which may achieve and cherish a just and lasting peace among ourselves, and with all nations."

Washington, D.C.
March 4, 1865

Top: (left) Lincoln, "The Lawyer" (right) Servius Tullius Stone
Beneath Statue on Superstructure
Bottom: (left) Lincoln, "The President" (right) Lincoln, "The
Emancipator"

In the East corridor, which leads to the sarcophagus chamber, or posterior rotunda, four niches hold bronze statuettes depicting four phases of Lincoln's career: Lincoln, the Ranger, Lincoln, the Soldier, Lincoln, the Circuit Rider, Lincoln, the Debater. Four more phases of his career are found in niches in the West or exit corridor: Lincoln, the Lawyer, Lincoln, the Candidate, Lincoln, the President, Lincoln, the Emancipator.

A red marble cenotaph is located in the center of the Sarcophagus chamber and carries this inscription:

ABRAHAM LINCOLN
1809–1865

On the north wall of the posterior rotunda, above a stained-glass window, is this inscription, carved in black marble:

"NOW HE BELONGS
TO THE AGES"

Nine flags form a semicircle behind the sarcophagus. Seven represent the states in which the Lincoln family travelled and lived — Massachusetts, New Jersey, Pennsylvania, Virginia, Kentucky, Indiana, and Illinois. The National Colors and the President's flag complete the group.

The grille covering the sarcophagus chamber window on the outside supports the name: LINCOLN.

Behind the south wall of the sarcophagus chamber are crypts where rest the remains of Mrs. Lincoln and three of her four sons:

MARY TODD
LINCOLN
1818–1882
Edward (Eddie) Baker
Lincoln
1846–1850
William (Willie) Wallace
Lincoln
1850–1862
Thomas (Tad)
Lincoln
1853–1871
Robert Todd
Lincoln
1843–1926
Buried in Arlington
National Cemetery

ANDREW JOHNSON

PRESIDENT OF
TWENTY-FIVE STATES

Grave of Andrew Johnson

ANDREW JOHNSON
1865–1869

The monument marking the grave of Andrew Johnson, the seventeenth President of the United States, is located in the Andrew Johnson National Cemetery, Greeneville, Tennessee, the Andrew Johnson National Historic site, administered by the National Park Service. Originally, the cemetery, consisting of fifteen acres, was owned by Andrew Johnson. It is now known as Monument Hill.

The monument is a marble shaft twenty-five feet in height. It is adorned by the figure of an American eagle, poised for flight.

Beneath the feet of the eagle and draping the upper third of the shaft is a carving of the flag of the Republic.

Near the base of the shaft is a scroll-like carving on which is written:

Constitution

of the

United States

Just beneath the scroll is an open Bible, upon the right side of which is superimposed the sculpture of a hand.

Flanking the scroll and Bible are two torches. The torch on the monument's right is plain while the other is ornamented with handles.

The base of the monument bears these inscriptions:

ANDREW JOHNSON
SEVENTEENTH PRESIDENT
OF THE UNITED STATES
Born Dec. 29, 1808
Died July 31, 1875
His Faith in the People Never Wavered

Eliza Johnson
Born Oct. 4, 1810
Died Jan. 19, 1876
In memory of our
Father and Mother

ULYSSES SIMPSON GRANT

PRESIDENT OF
THIRTY-EIGHT STATES

Ulysses S. Grant Mausoleum

ULYSSES SIMPSON GRANT
1869–1877

A massive mausoleum, located on Riverside Drive, New York City, is the monument marking the grave of Ulysses Simpson Grant, the eighteenth President of the United States.

Its exterior construction is of Maine gray granite with a white marble interior. The square base is ninety feet on each side and is seventy two feet high. A circular dome, forty-four feet in diameter, supported by twenty-four Ionic columns, crowns the structure.

The square base is surmounted by three circular sections, the lower two of which are of equal height. The center circular section is formed by a colonnade of twenty-four Ionic columns. On the parapet of the portico of the base section, between two carved figures representing War and Peace, is this inscription:

LET US HAVE PEACE

The monument is approached from the street level over a broad plaza. On either side of the seventy-foot-wide stairway leading to the entrance are flag poles. The pole on the East flies the four-star flag of the General of the Army and is in memory of Brigadier General Horace K. Porter, a member of General Grant's staff. The pole on the West flies the National Colors and is in memory of Major General Frederick Dent Grant, eldest son of President Grant.

On either side of the first flight of ten steps is a granite American eagle in flight.

A second flight of eight steps ends on a landing supporting six fluted Doric columns, each twenty-four feet high.

A third flight of two steps has its landing supporting four fluted Doric columns and two sixteen foot by five and one half foot bronze doors guarding the entrance.

Above the entrance is inscribed:

ULYSSES S. GRANT
BORN — APRIL–XXVII–MDCCCXXII
DIED — JULY–XXIII–MDCCCLXXXV

The outer walls of the East, West, and North walls of the square base each contain four fluted Doric columns.

The dome is reached by a circular stairway located to the left of the entrance and is one hundred fifty feet above street level.

A circular marble balustrade overlooks the crypt which contains the elevated sarcophagi of President and Mrs. Grant. As observed from above, the sarcophagus on the left is inscribed:

Ulysses
S.
Grant

The sarcophagus on the right is inscribed:

Julia
D.
Grant

Opposite the entrance is a marble stairway, which divides half way to the lower level so that the crypt may be entered along the West wall or along the East wall. On either side of this stairway in the Memorial Hall is a trophy room. The walls of these rooms are covered by maps of the United States showing the location of the battles of the Civil War, with significant markers to indicate those participated in by General Grant.

Battle flags, contained in cases in each room, represent Volunteer regiments from Illinois, Ohio, Pennsylvania, Iowa, New York, Indiana, Missouri, and Wisconsin.

At the top of the stairs, the National Colors are flanked by the state flags of Ohio and Illinois.

The nine-ton sarcophagi of Wisconsin porphyry, gray maroon in color, are located in the center of the circular crypt, equidistant from the floor of the crypt and the top of the balustrade from which visitors view the last resting place of the great Civil War general.

In the niches around the outer wall of the crypt, in a counter-clockwise direction from the stairway entering the crypt, are heroic busts of General Grant's most trusted field generals:

Philip Henry Sheridan
1831–1888, West Point 1853
William Tecumseh Sherman
1820–1901, West Point 1840
James Birdseye McPherson
1828–1864, West Point 1853
Edward Otho Cresap Ord
1818–1883, West Point 1839
George Henry Thomas
1816–1870, West Point 1840

Three of the four arched extensions of the Memorial Room contain lunettes of Grant's spectacular military victories in the War Between the States. The one on the West wall depicts Grant and Thomas contemplating the victories during the Chattanooga, Lookout Mountain, and Missionary Ridge campaigns. The one on the East wall symbolizes Grant, Sherman, and McPherson in the Forts Henry and Donelson, the Shiloh, Corinth, and Vicksburg campaigns.

The lunette on the North wall symbolizes Sheridan and Ord in the Petersburg-Appomattox campaign, and General Grant accepting General Lee's surrender at Appomattox.

In the triangles formed by the joining arches and the base of the rotunda are panels in bas-relief representing the career of Ulysses S. Grant.

At the junction of the South and West walls, two seated figures support the tree of life. The right hand of one allegorical figure holds an open book while the left hand of the other holds a torch. This represents his early life and education.

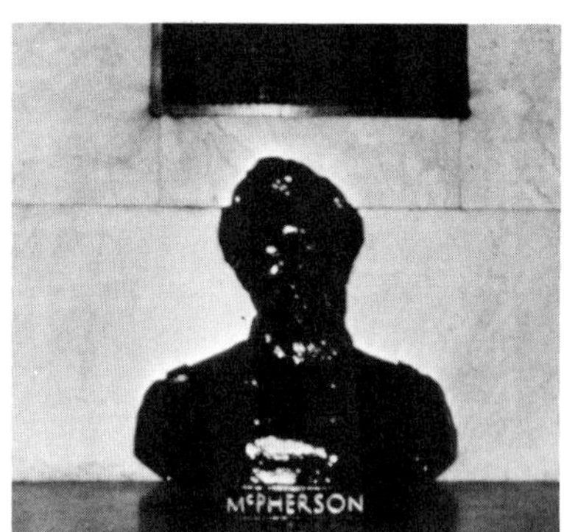

Busts of Union Generals: General Thomas, General Ord, General Sheridan, General McPherson, General Sherman

At the junction of the East and North walls, two seated allegorical figures support a sword. The left hand of one figure holds a helmet while the right hand of the other holds a shield. This bas-relief represents Grant's military career during the Mexican War and the Civil War.

At the junction of the West and North walls, two seated allegorical figures hold a bundle of rods enclosing a double ax. This fasces was the symbol of civil power during the Presidency of General Grant.

One of the figures holds in her left hand a cornucopia and the other figure holds in her right hand an olive branch. This panel represents Grant's administration as one of peace and prosperity.

At the junction of the West and South walls, two semi-seated allegorical figures support an extinguished lamp. The left hand of one holds a globe surmounted by an angel with the scales of justice, while the right hand of the other holds a sprig of laurel. This bas-relief represents the death of General Grant.

Above the lunettes and midway to the dome of the rotunda there is a circular colonnade, each column of which is crowned by an American eagle with outstretched wings.

Immediately behind the mausoleum, and at the site of Grant's temporary grave, is a plot of ground surrounded by an iron fence. Within the enclosure are two trees, one a ginko tree and the other a Chinese cork tree.

The bronze plaque bears this inscription:

This tree is planted
At the side of the tomb of
GENERAL U. S. GRANT
Ex-President of the

United States of America
For the purpose
Of commemorating his
Greatness by
LI HUNG CHANG
Guardian of the Prince
Grand Secretary of State
Earl of the First Order
YANG YU
Envoy Extraordinary
And Minister
Plenipotentiary of China
Vice President
Of the Board of Censors
KWANG HSU 23rd year
4th Moon, May 1897

Sarcophagi of General and Mrs. Grant

RUTHERFORD BIRCHARD HAYES

PRESIDENT OF
THIRTY-EIGHT STATES

Grave of President and Mrs. Hayes

RUTHERFORD B. HAYES
1877–1881

A Vermont granite monument marks the grave of Rutherford B. Hayes, the Nineteenth President of the United States.

It is located in Spiegel Grove of the Hayes Homestead in Fremont, Ohio. The inscription reads:

RUTHERFORD BIRCHARD HAYES
October 4, 1822 — January 17, 1893
LUCY WEBB HAYES
August 27, 1831 — June 25, 1889

Webb Cook Hayes, the second son of President and Mrs. Hayes, is buried to the rear of the President's monument. Colonel Hayes, as a member of the Ohio National Guard on duty in the Philippines in 1899, was awarded the Congressional Medal of Honor.

A large slab of native stone, flush with the turf of the "Knoll," is inscribed:

Colonel
Webb Cook Hayes
M.H.
March 20, 1856   July 26, 1934
Mary Miller Hayes
April 11, 1856   March 3, 1935

A replica of the Congressional Medal of Honor adorns the grave.

President Hayes was originally buried in the Oakwood Cemetery where many of his children are buried.

Courtesy of Ohio Historical Society

Courtesy of Rutherford B. Hayes Library

Top: Rear View of Hayes Monument
Bottom: Graves of Colonel and Mrs. Webb Cook Hayes

JAMES ABRAM GARFIELD

PRESIDENT OF
THIRTY-EIGHT STATES

Garfield Mausoleum

JAMES ABRAM GARFIELD
March 4, 1881–September 19, 1881

The Garfield Memorial Mausoleum is located in the Lake View Cemetery, Cleveland, Ohio. Built of native sandstone, it consists of a circular tower fifty feet in diameter and one hundred eighty feet high. At the base of the tower projects a square porch whose parapets, externally, contain five panels of life-sized bas-reliefs representing the career of Garfield: (L to R as one faces the monument) Teacher, Statesman and Orator, Soldier (Hero of Chickamauga), Taking the Oath as President, and His Body Lying in State in the Rotunda of the Capitol.

Circular stairs on either side of the porch lead to the balcony behind the parapet.

From the vaulted vestibule of the porch, whose pavement is of stone mosaic, entry is made into the memorial chapel. The chapel is circular in form. Arranged in a semicircle are ten red granite columns supporting a rich marble mosaic frieze. These columns also support the beautiful dome of the chapel which is decorated with winged figures representing North, South, East, and West. A band of wreaths, alternately of laurel and immortelles, are emblematic of earthly glory and Heavenly immortality.

The frieze depicts the funeral procession. The center panel, opposite the chapel entrance, shows Columbia and her daughter States in grief around the bier. Processions on the right have allegorical figures representing "Law," "Justice," "Concord." Processions on the left have allegorical figures representing "War," "Literature," "Labor," and "Veterans."

Over the entrance doorway within the chapel, on either side, are seated figures in glass mosaic signifying "War" and "Peace." The inscription beneath these mosaics reads:

Courtesy of Lake View Cemetery

Statue of President Garfield

"Erected by a grateful Country in memory of
James Abram Garfield, 20th President
of the United States of America,
Scholar, Soldier, Statesman, Patriot;
Born 19th Nov. 1831, Died 19th Sept. 1881"

Outside the columns of the chapel is a circular aisle. This corridor separates the dias of sectile mosaic in designs of rare and nameless marble from the outer circular wall of the tower.

On the dias, in pure white Carrara marble is an heroic statue of Garfield standing in front of a chair. The chair represents the one he occupied in Congress.

In the outer wall of the circular corridor are ten stained-glass windows, one each to represent Massachusetts, Rhode Island, Connecticut, New York, New Jersey, Pennsylvania, Delaware, Virginia, North Carolina, and South Carolina, and four window-like panels representing Ohio, New Hampshire, Georgia, and Maryland. These states represent the original thirteen plus Ohio.

Beneath the chapel is the Crypt containing the sarcophagi of James Abram Garfield and his wife, Lucretia R. Garfield.

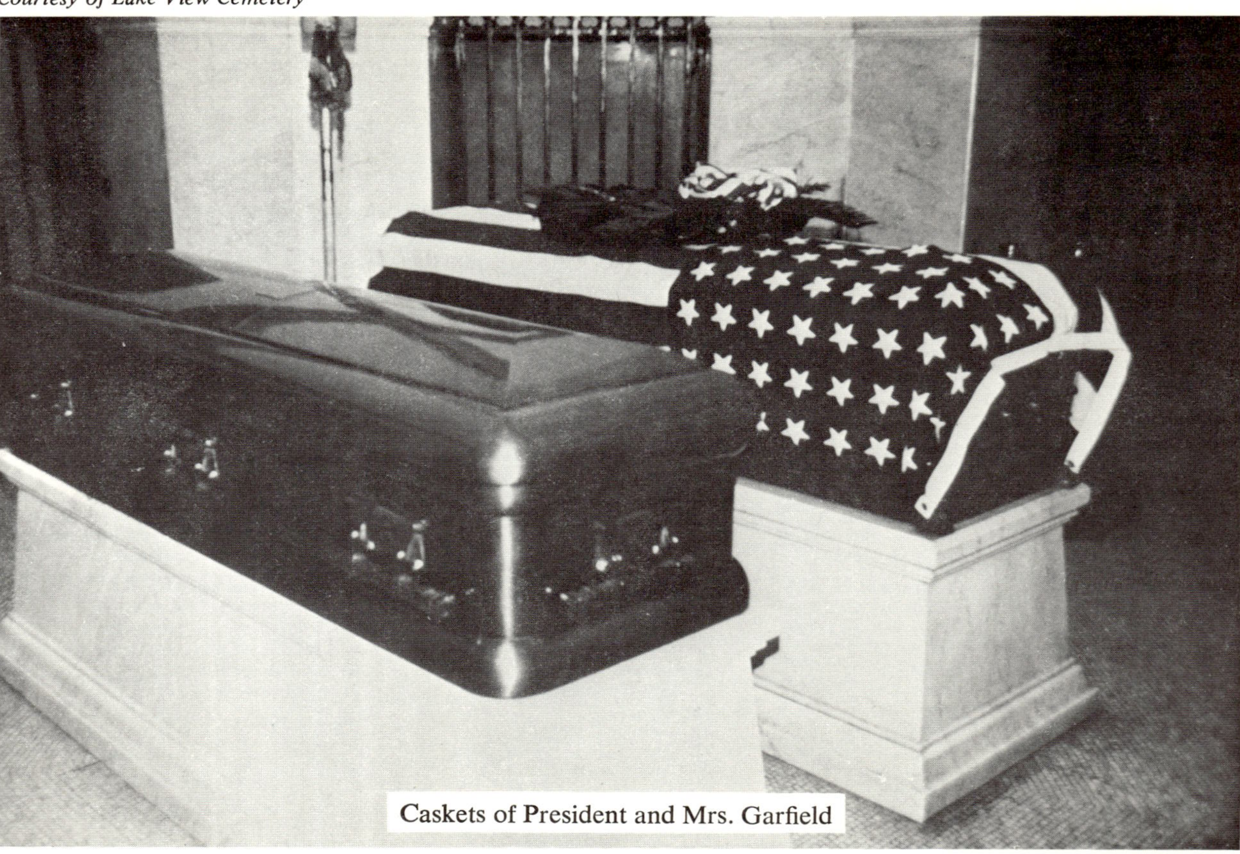

Caskets of President and Mrs. Garfield

Stained-Glass Windows: Top (from left) Ohio, New York, Maryland, (center) War and Peace, Bottom (from left) Georgia, North Carolina, New Hampshire

Stained-Glass Windows: Top (from left) Connecticut, Rhode Island, Pennsylvania, Virginia, Bottom (from left) Delaware, Massachusetts, New Jersey, South Carolina

CHESTER ALAN ARTHUR

PRESIDENT OF
THIRTY-EIGHT STATES

Sarcophagus of Chester Alan Arthur

CHESTER ALAN ARTHUR
1881–1885

The monument marking the grave of Chester Alan Arthur, the twenty-first President of the United States, is located in the Albany Rural Cemetery, Menands-Watervliet, New York.

The burial plot is approached by five white granite steps. Each copestone of the walls of the steps is ornamented by bronze urns.

With the Napoleon sarcophagus for its motif, the memorial has excellent proportions, and its plain and highly polished dark Quincy granite makes it impressive. A feeling of awe and inspiration is elicited by the bronze Angel of Bereavement standing by the pedestal at the head of the sarcophagus. Her left hand, palm up, extends along the four-sided roof and is placing on the tomb the palm branch of victory. This last symbolic earthly tribute sweeps over the foot of the memorial and bends gracefully downward over the end.

The Angel's right arm hangs extended by her side, with her hand touching one of the bronze wings.

On the front of the base, between the supporting black granite pedestals of the sarcophagus, is the word:

ARTHUR

A bronze plaque, attached to the top of the base just in front of the rear pedestal, bears this inscription:

CHESTER ALAN ARTHUR
21st President of the United States
Born, October 5, 1830; Died, November 18, 1886

Behind the Sarcophagus is a seven-foot by one and one-half foot rectangular white granite stone. Superimposed thereon is the sword and cross of a crusader. Around the border is this inscription:

Top: Approach to Arthur Cemetery Plot
Bottom: Grave of Mrs. Chester Alan Arthur

"Here lies the Body of Ellen Lewis Herndon, Wife of
Chester Alan Arthur
Born at Culpeper, C.H., Virginia, August 30, 1837. Died at
New York, Jan. 12, AD 1880"

An adjoining stone reads:
Chester Alan Arthur II, Son of Chester Alan Arthur &
Ellen Lewis Herndon
Born at New York City July 25, 1864
Rowena Dashwood, Second wife of Chester Alan Arthur II
Born at Colorado Springs November 8, 1894
Died at Colorado Springs November 5, 1965

Chester Alan Arthur III, son of Chester Alan Arthur II &
Myra Townsend Fithian, born at Colorado Springs
March 21, 1901

STEPHEN GROVER CLEVELAND

PRESIDENT OF
THIRTY-EIGHT STATES
AND
FORTY-FIVE STATES

Grave of Grover Cleveland

GROVER CLEVELAND
1885–1889
1893–1897

The monument marking the grave of Grover Cleveland, the twenty-second and the twenty-fourth President of the United States, is located in the Princeton Cemetery, Princeton, New Jersey. It consists of nearly a square block of smooth granite surmounted by an urn-shaped finial. The inscription reads:

GROVER CLEVELAND
Born, Caldwell, New Jersey
March 18, 1837
Died, Princeton, New Jersey
June 24,
1908

A headstone nearby contains the following:
Ruth Cleveland
Daughter of
Grover Cleveland
and
Frances Folsom Cleveland
October 3, 1891
January 7, 1904

BENJAMIN HARRISON

PRESIDENT OF
FORTY-FOUR STATES

Graves of President and Mrs. Benjamin Harrison

BENJAMIN HARRISON
1889–1893

The grave of Benjamin Harrison, the twenty-third President of the United States, is located in the Crown Hill Cemetery, Indianapolis, Indiana. A monument of chaste symmetry is inscribed:

BENJAMIN HARRISON
August 20, 1833
March 1, 1901
Lawyer and Publicist
Colonel 70th Regiment Ind. Volunteers
1861–1865
Breveted Brigadier General 1865
U.S. Senator 1881–1887
President 1889–1893
"Statesman, yet friend to man: of soul sincere
In action faithful, and in honor clear".*

As one faces the monument, the headstone on the left reads:

Benjamin Harrison

As one faces the monument, the headstone on the right reads:

Caroline Scott
Harrison

*Quotation from Pope's "An Epistle to Mr. Addison" beginning with the 67th line.

WILLIAM McKINLEY

PRESIDENT OF
FORTY-FIVE STATES

Courtesy of Ohio Historical Society

McKinley Mausoleum

WILLIAM McKINLEY
1897–1901

The monument marking the last resting place of William McKinley, twenty-fifth President of the United States, is located on Monument Hill, east of the Westlawn Cemetery in Canton, Ohio. It is approached by four flights of twenty-three steps.

On the second landing is a bronze statue of William McKinley, the base of which bears this inscription:

William McKinley
President
of the
United States
A statesman singularly
Gifted to unite discord-
Ant forces of Government
And mould the diverse pur-
Poses of men toward a progress-
Ive and Salutary Action —
A Magistrate whose poise
Of judgment was tested and
Vindicated in a succession
Of National Emergencies —
Good Citizen — Brave Soldier —
Wise Executive — Helper and
Leader of Men — Exemplar to
His People of the Virtues
That Build and Conserve the
State, Society, and the Home.

The circular mass building, without windows, springs from a circular platform located on the fourth landing. This platform is one hundred seventy-five feet in diameter. On this platform is placed the chapel of the mausoleum, the external diameter of which is seventy-five feet. Two thirds of the distance to the dome, the walls narrow to an interior diameter of fifty feet. The dome carries a circular window that is seventy-seven feet from the floor.

These two concentric masonry drums are inclined inward, diminishing in diameter as they ascend to the concave roof. Between the dome opening, or oculus, and the smaller drum, is a secondary cornice in which forty-five stars are set. These stars represent the States of the Republic at the time of the death of William McKinley.

The internal arrangement of the mortuary chapel or chamber features a Greek cross. This is made possible by four recesses or bays in the lower portion of the tower.

At the intersection of the arms of the cross are located the sarcophagi. The sarcophagi are made from one block of dark green Windsor, Vermont granite. The ends face the entrance and have gold plated letters which read:

WILLIAM McKINLEY   IDA McKINLEY

The sarcophagi rest on "bearers" whose ends are carved Lions' heads. The bearers in turn rest upon a base of polished "Black Berlin" granite from Wisconsin. The sarcophagi and the socle are supported by a parapet of Grey Eagle Tennessee marble.

The four bays are arched recesses flanked by Doric columns. These eight columns support a circular entablature bearing the inscription:

LET US EVER REMEMBER THAT OUR IN-
TEREST IS IN CONCORD, NOT CONFLICT,
AND THAT OUR REAL EMINENCE RESTS IN
THE VICTORIES OF PEACE, NOT THOSE OF
WAR.

Statue of President McKinley

Each keystone of the arched recesses of each bay bears thirteen stripes and each keystone supports an eagle preparing for flight.

An attic is formed from pilasters above the columns, and there are recessed panels between the pilasters. An inverted torch is placed at each end of the panels, signifying death.

The facade, in which the entrance door is located, is a rectangular pavilion extending two thirds of the height of the mausoleum. A panel near the top of the pavilion, as one enters, is inscribed:

1843   IN MEMORIAM   1901
William McKinley
PRESIDENT OF THE UNITED STATES

In the arch just above the entrance door, a panel in bas-relief, depicts the Republic, symbolically, with a seated female figure whose outstretched arms are above a kneeling youth on her right laying a sword and shield at her feet, and another kneeling youth on her left holding the products of industry.

This lunette symbolizes the protection Mother Republic extends to everything worthy in peace, prosperity, and industry. The wreaths on the sword and shield on one side are the laurels of victory, while on the other, there are symbols of prosperity and industry.

Courtesy of Ohio Historical Society

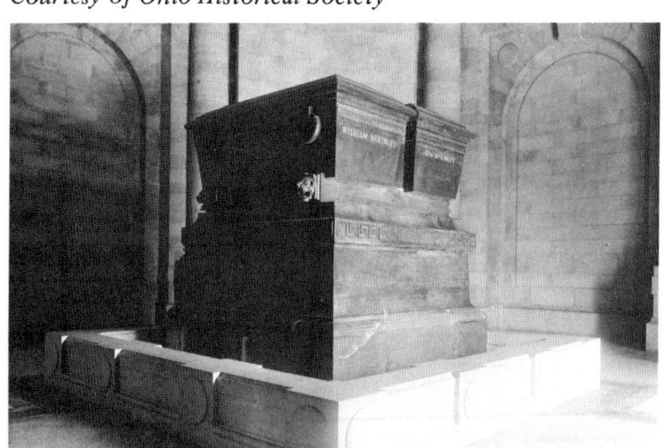

Sarcophagi of President and Mrs. McKinley

THEODORE ROOSEVELT

PRESIDENT OF
FORTY-SIX STATES

Grave of President and Mrs. Theodore Roosevelt

THEODORE ROOSEVELT
1901–1909

The monument marking the grave of Theodore Roosevelt, the twenty-sixth President of the United States, is located in Youngs Memorial Cemetery, Oyster Bay, New York. It consists of a headstone framed by fluted pilasters supporting a concave moulding. Beneath the moulding, on the slab, is the Presidential seal.

The inscription reads:

THEODORE ROOSEVELT
Born October 27, 1858
Died January 6, 1919
and his wife
EDITH KERMIT
Born August 6, 1861
Died September 30, 1948

WILLIAM HOWARD TAFT

PRESIDENT OF
FORTY-EIGHT STATES

Courtesy of Arlington National Cemetery, Dept. of the Army

Grave of President and Mrs. William Howard Taft

WILLIAM HOWARD TAFT
1909–1913

The monument marking the grave of William Howard Taft, the twenty-seventh President of the United States, is located in the Arlington National Cemetery, Arlington, Virginia.

The red granite shaft is twelve feet high and is the replica of a tall, simple Greek stele, dating from the fourth century B.C.

The monument is surmounted by an anthemion. This ornamentation is double concave in form. Its beautifully carved leaves resemble those of the acanthus or the Assyrian palmette.

Beneath the moulding of the upright slab are two carved rosettes. The monument was designed by Bryant Baker, who was the sculptor of a bust of President Taft.

The stele bears the following inscription:

WILLIAM HOWARD

TAFT

1857–1930

PRESIDENT

OF THE

UNITED STATES

*   *   *

CHIEF JUSTICE

OF THE

UNITED STATES

———

His Wife

HELEN HERRON

1861   1943

THOMAS WOODROW WILSON

PRESIDENT OF
FORTY-EIGHT STATES

Sarcophagus of Woodrow Wilson from Wilson Bay

WOODROW WILSON
1913–1921

The monument marking the grave of Woodrow Wilson, the twenty-eighth President of the United States, is located in the Wilson Bay of the Washington Cathedral, the Cathedral of St. Peter and St. Paul (Episcopal), Mt. Saint Alban, Washington, D.C.

The Wilson Bay is a portion of the south aisle of the nave of the cathedral. The north face of the sarcophagus is incorporated in the structure of the Bay arch and contains the seals in stone of the three institutions headed by Woodrow Wilson during his career: Princeton University, the United States, and the State of New Jersey.

On top of the tomb is the crusader's sword, ornamented by thistles, symbolic of Scotland. Parallel with the sword is this inscription:

WOODROW WILSON
1856   1924

At the foot of the sarcophagus, on the east wall, is inscribed:

IN LOVING MEMORY
OF
EDITH BOLLING WILSON
1872   1961
BURIED IN THE VAULT
BENEATH THIS BAY

On the east wall, in a niche above the entrance arch of the bay, is a figure of St. Andrew (the patron saint of Scotland). The corbel below represents the Presbyterian manse in Staunton, Virginia, where he was born, December 28, 1856.

177

On the east wall, south of the entrance arch to the Wilson
Bay, are these inscriptions:

This is not a day of triumph, it is
A day of dedication. Here meet
Not the forces of party, but the
Forces of humanity. Men's hearts
Wait upon us; men's lives hang in
The balance. Who shall live up to
the great trust? Who dare fail
to try?

Ist Inaugural Address

The right is more precious than
Peace and we shall fight for the
Things which we have always
Carried nearest our hearts — for
Democracy. For the right of those
Who submit to authority to have
A voice in their own government,
For the rights and liberties of
Small nations, for a Universal
Dominion of right by such a con-
cert of free peoples as shall
Bring peace and safety to all
Nations and make the world it-
self at last free.

War Message To Congress

On the west wall, in a niche above the exit arch of the bay,
is the figure of John Calvin, the founder of Presbyterianism.
The corbel below symbolizes Nassau Hall, with the academic
ivy of Princeton University.

Wilson Sarcophagus from Cathedral Nave

The west wall contains the following inscriptions:

> The stage is set, the destiny
>   disclosed. It has come about by
>   no plan of our conceiving, but
>   by the hand of God who led us
>   into the way. We cannot turn
>   back. We can only go forward
> with lifted eyes and freshen-
>   ed spirit to follow the vision.
>   It was of this that we dreamed
>   at our birth. America shall in
>   truth show the way. The light
>   streams upon the path ahead,
>   and nowhere else.
>
> *Submission of Peace Treaty*
> *to Senate*

*   *   *

> The sum of the whole matter
>   is this, that our Civilization can-
> not survive materially unless
>   it be redeemed spiritually. It can
>   be saved only by becoming perme-
>   ated with the spirit of Christ —
>   and being made free and happy
>   by the practices which spring
> out of that spirit
>
> *Last Published Words*

In the center of the multi-colored marble floor of the Wilson Bay is an eighteen inches in diameter bronze seal of the President of the United States.

The stained-glass lancets of the outer wall of the bay are devoted to themes of War and Peace.

Woodrow Wilson died February 3, 1924 and was initially buried in the Bethlehem Chapel of the Washington Cathedral. His body was interred in the Wilson Bay December 28, 1956.

WARREN GAMALIEL HARDING

PRESIDENT OF
FORTY-EIGHT STATES

Harding Mausoleum Exterior

WARREN G. HARDING
1921–1923

Warren G. Harding, the twenty-ninth President of the United States, is buried in Marion, Ohio.

The monument marking his grave is a replica of the Greek peristyle formed externally by a colonnade of twenty-four stately Doric columns of white Georgia marble, one hundred five feet in diameter.

The columns are twenty-eight feet high, average six feet in diameter and support a circular entablature sixteen feet high.

The entire structure is fifty-two feet above ground level. It can be approached from any direction at its base by two flights of four steps. Each step is one foot high and one and one half feet wide. A marble walk, seven and one half feet wide, marks the first landing. The second landing provides support for the Doric columns which are seven feet in diameter at the base, tapering gracefully to five feet in diameter at the summit.

Immediately behind the massive Doric columns is a solid wall of marble, not attached to the entablature, and extending three fourths of the circumference of the mausoleum. The open portion, or entrance, is behind six of the Doric columns. Directly opposite the Temple entrance, north, on the solid wall is this inscription:

WARREN GAMALIEL HARDING
Twenty-ninth President of the United States
Born Nov. 2, 1865   Died Aug. 2, 1923
FLORENCE KLING HARDING
Born Aug. 15, 1860   Died Nov. 21, 1924

Within the circular court, without shelter, are the sarcophagi of President and Mrs. Harding, each covered by a nine-foot by four-foot by one-foot emerald pearl (black) Labrador granite slab.

The tomb on the left, as one faces the graves, is ornamented by a bronze wreath of palm leaves, indicating the last resting place of Warren G. Harding.

The other is ornamented by a bronze wreath of roses, marking the grave of Mrs. Harding.

A four-foot wide marble walk of grey alternated by white squares surrounds the grave-site. Around the inner border of the walk are twenty fluted Ionic columns, each twenty feet in height. The eight-foot high entablature forms the inner wall of a terrace or hanging garden. Its outer wall is formed by the wall of the mausoleum. The resulting cloister begins and ends with two Ionic columns.

Trees, shrubs, vines, and other plantings surround the graves, and enrich the roof of the cloister.

A seven-foot high iron fence separates the inner walk from the outer circle of massive pillars at the entrance.

Courtesy of Harding Memorial Association

Graves of President and Mrs. Harding Inside the Mausoleum

CALVIN COOLIDGE

PRESIDENT OF
FORTY-EIGHT STATES

Graves of President and Mrs. Coolidge

CALVIN COOLIDGE
1923–1929

An unpretentious headstone dominated by the Seal of the President of the United States marks the grave of Calvin Coolidge, the thirtieth President of the United States.

The monument is located in the Village Cemetery at Plymouth Notch, Vermont and is inscribed:

CALVIN COOLIDGE
JULY 4, 1872
JANUARY 5, 1933

To the right of President Coolidge's headstone is a smaller headstone, the same in design. A wreath replaces the Seal of the President of the United States. The headstone carries this inscription:

CALVIN
COOLIDGE
JUNIOR

*   *   *

April 13, 1908
July 7, 1924

As one faces the grave of President Coolidge, the headstone of Mrs. Coolidge is located on the left. This headstone is of the same size and design as that of the President.

A wreath replaces the Presidential Seal.

The tombstone bears the following inscription:

GRACE A. GOODHUE
WIFE OF
CALVIN COOLIDGE
January 3, 1879
July 8, 1957

A State of Vermont historical marker records the following:

CALVIN COOLIDGE

1872   1933
Born July 4, 1872 in a house back
of store, Calvin Coolidge from 4
years of age lived in the Homestead
across the road, now owned by the
State of Vermont. Here on Aug. 3,
1923 he was inaugurated President
and here he spent many vacations.
In the Notch Cemetery he rests
beside his wife & son and 4
generations of forebears.

Top: Coolidge Row in Village Cemetery
Bottom: Calvin Coolidge Historical Marker

HERBERT CLARK HOOVER

PRESIDENT OF
FORTY-EIGHT STATES

Burial Plot of President and Mrs. Hoover

HERBERT CLARK HOOVER
1929 — 1933

The grave of Herbert Clark Hoover, the thirty-first President of the United States, is located on a grassy mound at the Overlook, a portion of his birthplace property, West Branch, Iowa.

Two plain flat slabs of Vermont marble, each measuring ten feet two inches by four feet six inches by one foot, and each weighing four thousand pounds, form the monument marking the grave sites of President and Mrs. Hoover.

The last resting place is approached from the left by a curved walk.

The corner marker of the plot on the left is a large, square block of Vermont marble, in chaste symmetry, the front of which is inscribed:

HERBERT HOOVER
1874 — 1964

This same inscription appears on the top of the marble slab covering his grave.

The corner marker of the plot on the right is a large, square block of Vermont marble, in chaste symmetry, the front of which is inscribed:

LOU HENRY HOOVER
1874 — 1944

The same inscription is found on the top of the marble slab covering her grave.

Designated a National Historic Site

Graves of President and Mrs. Hoover

FRANKLIN DELANO ROOSEVELT

PRESIDENT OF
FORTY-EIGHT STATES

Grave of President and Mrs. Franklin D. Roosevelt

FRANKLIN DELANO ROOSEVELT
1933–1945

A massive block of marble marks the grave of Franklin Delano Roosevelt, located on the National Historic Site of Hyde Park, New York. He was the thirty-second President of the United States.

The marble of the monument, known as "Imperial Danby," was quarried in Vermont. It is eight feet long, four feet wide, and three feet high. It rests on a marble base extending two feet beyond the monument on all sides.

The following inscription is found on the south side of the monument:

FRANKLIN DELANO ROOSEVELT
1882 — 1945
ANNA ELEANOR ROOSEVELT
1884 — 1962

Designated a National Historic Site

DWIGHT DAVID EISENHOWER

PRESIDENT OF
FIFTY STATES

Place of Meditation

DWIGHT DAVID EISENHOWER
1953–1961

The last resting place of Dwight David Eisenhower, the thirty-fourth President of the United States, is located in the Place of Meditation (The Eisenhower Chapel) situated on the Eisenhower Center Grounds, Abilene, Kansas. The tomb is recessed. The forward half of the crypt is guarded by a wrought-iron fence and the rear portion is enclosed by eight-foot high Travertine marble panels. This portion of the tomb is flanked by shrubbery with a tiny fountain and pool between.

A blue velvet drapery on the rear panel hangs below a walnut cross and extends downward toward the pool. In gold letters is inscribed his Inaugural Prayer of January 20, 1953:

> "Almighty God, as we stand here at this moment, my future associates in the Executive branch of government join me in beseeching that Thou will make full and complete our dedication to the service of the the people in this throng, and their fellow citizens everywhere.
>
> Give us, we pray, the power to discern clearly right from wrong, and allow all our words and actions to be governed thereby, and by the laws of this land. Especially we pray that our concern shall be for all the people regardless of station, race, or calling.
>
> May cooperation be permitted and be the mutual aim of those, who, under the concepts of our Constitution, hold to differing political faiths, so that all may work for the good of our beloved country and Thy glory. Amen."

Sanctuary of the Eisenhower Chapel

Marking the grave of President Eisenhower is a one-foot square bronze plaque bearing this inscription:

DWIGHT DAVID
EISENHOWER
BORN OCTOBER 14, 1890
DIED MARCH 25, 1969

To the right of the President's grave marker is a one-foot square bronze plaque which reads:

DOUD DWIGHT
EISENHOWER
BORN SEPTEMBER 24, 1917
DIED JANUARY 2, 1921

Designated a National Historic Site

Top: Grave of President Eisenhower
Bottom: Eisenhower Crypt

JOHN FITZGERALD KENNEDY

PRESIDENT OF
FIFTY STATES

John Fitzgerald Kennedy Burial Plot Below General
Robert E. Lee Mansion

JOHN FITZGERALD KENNEDY
1961–1963

The monument marking the grave of John Fitzgerald Kennedy, the thirty-fifth President of the United States, is located in the Arlington National Cemetery, Arlington, Virginia.

The concrete pavement surrounding the flat black granite slab with its cobblestone-like border, and the eternal flame form a Greek cross. The Slab and the Eternal Flame are flush with the ground level and are located at the intersection of the horizontal and vertical arms of the Greek cross.

The Slab is inscribed:

JOHN FITZGERALD KENNEDY
1917–1963

and is ornamented with a Latin cross.

The esplanade portion of the monument is elliptical in shape. Concrete and granite blocks forming the rim of the Esplanade bear quotations from President Kennedy's inaugural address of January 20, 1961.

The following inscriptions are on the Esplanade of the monument:

Let the word go forth
From this time and place
To friends and foe alike
That the torch has been passed
To a new generation of Americans

Let every nation know
Whether it wishes us well or ill
That we shall pay any price * bear any burden
Meet any hardship * support any friend
Oppose any foe to assure the survival
And the success of liberty

Now the trumpet summons us again
Not as a call to bear arms * though embattled we are
But a call to bear the burden of a long twilight struggle
A struggle against the common enemies of man
Tyranny * Poverty * Disease * And War Itself

In the long history of the world
Only a few generations have been granted
The role of defending freedom
In the hour of maximum danger
I do not shrink from this opportunity
I welcome it

The Energy * The Faith * The Devotion
Which we bring to this endeavor
Will light our country
And all who serve it
And the glow from that fire
Can truly light the world

And so My Fellow Americans
Ask not what your country can do for you
Ask what you can do for your country
My Fellow Citizens of the World * Ask not
What America will do for you * but what together
We can do for the freedom of man

With a good conscience our only sure reward
With history the final judge of our deeds
Let us go forth to lead the land we love * Asking his
    blessing
And his help * But knowing that here on earth
God's work must truly be our own

Grave of President Kennedy

APPENDIX

Summary of the Burial Places of the Presidents

Enshrined in Churches or Chapels
    John Adams
    John Quincy Adams
    Thomas Woodrow Wilson
    Dwight David Eisenhower*

Buried on Own Estate
    George Washington
    Thomas Jefferson
    James Madison
    Andrew Jackson
    William Henry Harrison
    Rutherford Birchard Hayes
    Herbert Clark Hoover*
    Franklin Delano Roosevelt*

Buried in Family Cemeteries now National Cemeteries
    Malcolm Zachary Taylor
    Andrew Johnson*

Enshrined in a Mausoleum Erected by Popular
  Subscription
    Abraham Lincoln***
    Ulysses Simpson Grant**
    James Abram Garfield
    William McKinley
    Warren Gamaliel Harding

Buried in Arlington National Cemetery
    William Howard Taft
    John Fitzgerald Kennedy

Buried on State Capitol Grounds
  James Knox Polk

Buried in Public Cemeteries
  James Monroe
  Martin Van Buren
  John Tyler
  David Rice Atchison
  Millard Fillmore
  Franklin Pierce
  James Buchanan
  Jefferson Davis
  Chester Alan Arthur
  Stephen Grover Cleveland
  Benjamin Harrison
  Theodore Roosevelt
  Calvin Coolidge

  *Designated a National Historic Site
  **Designated a National Memorial
  ***Designated a National Historic Landmark

BIBLIOGRAPHY

1. *Graves of Our Presidents,* Edgar Stanley Martin, Lefax, Inc., Philadelphia, 1926.

2. *Presidential Shrines,* William Judson Hampton, Christopher Publishing House, Boston, 1928.

3. *History of Cemetery Sculpture Vol. 1,* Arnold Whittick Mineral Publications, Ltd., London, 1938.

HARRY S. TRUMAN

PRESIDENT OF
FORTY-EIGHT STATES

Truman Burial Plot

HARRY S. TRUMAN
April 12, 1945–January 20, 1953

The burial plot of Harry S. Truman, the thirty-third President of the United States, is located in the courtyard of the Harry S. Truman Library and Museum, Independence, Missouri.

The space allotted for graves, twelve feet by twelve feet, is surrounded by a pavement creating a square enclosure approximately thirty-three feet on each side. President Truman is buried in the north side of the plot with the top of the Memorial Ledger toward the West and the bottom toward the East.

The four paved walks leading to and from the burial plot may be symbolic of events in his life as he journeyed "toward the undiscovered country from whose bourne no traveller returns." The South path could represent his elective experiences in the Masonic Fraternity. The East path may symbolize his affiliation with many higher Masonic orders. The other East path could point the way to National offices. The West path may be symbolic of highlights as Senator, Vice-President, and President, and this path's northern extension may recall the Masonic honors he received.

The thirty-three feet square paved area may remind all of his election to the thirty-third Degree, Ancient Accepted Scottish Rite, Southern Jurisdiction. This hallowed ground of Harry S. Truman may be considered a Masonic Ocean — to which all Masonic Rivers ran and from which, henceforth, all provinces and continents of Masonic thought, ideals and distinguished service to country and to humanity receive their dew and rain.

Harry S. Truman Memorial Ledger

The inscription on the horizontal stone slab monument is as follows:

HARRY S. TRUMAN
BORN MAY 8, 1884
LAMAR, MISSOURI
DIED DECEMBER 26, 1972

MARRIED JUNE 28, 1919
DAUGHTER
BORN FEBRUARY 17, 1924

JUDGE
EASTERN DISTRICT
JACKSON COUNTY
JAN. 1, 1923 — JAN. 1, 1925
PRESIDING JUDGE
JACKSON COUNTY
JAN. 1, 1927 — JAN. 1, 1935
UNITED STATES SENATOR
MISSOURI
JAN. 3, 1935 — JAN. 18, 1945
VICE-PRESIDENT
UNITED STATES
JAN. 20, 1945 — APRIL 12, 1945
PRESIDENT
UNITED STATES
APRIL 12, 1945 — JAN. 20, 1953

The seal of the President of the United States is above the name Harry S. Truman and the Seal of the United States Senate and the Seal of Jackson County, Missouri are at the bottom of the Ledger on the right and left sides, respectively.

The Memorial Ledger is a white granite slab, eight feet long, three feet six inches in width, eight inches thick and weighs thirty-seven hundred pounds. The Presidential Seal has a three dimensional appearance. The edges of the slab are beveled.

LYNDON BAINES JOHNSON

PRESIDENT OF
FIFTY STATES

Courtesy of Lyndon B. Johnson Historic Site

Johnson Cemetery Entrance

On the stone wall of the cemetery, to the left of the iron gates guarding the entrance, is a bronze plaque which reads:

ELEGY WRITTEN IN A COUNTRY CHURCHYARD

> The curfew tolls the knell of parting day
> The lowing herd winds slowly o'er the lea,
> The ploughman homeward plods his weary way,
> And leaves the world to darkness and to me.

Verses from the Elegy written in a Country Churchyard are most appropriate for the Johnson Cemetery because they are reminiscent of the Stoke Poges churchyard of Thomas Gray.

The Grave of President Johnson

Courtesy of Lyndon B. Johnson Historic Site

"The boast of heraldry, the pomp of pow'r,
And all that beauty, all that wealth e'er gave,

Await alike th' inevitable hour:
The paths of glory lead but to the grave."

LYNDON BAINES JOHNSON
November 22, 1963–January 20, 1969

The monument marking the grave of Lyndon Baines Johnson, the thirty-sixth President of the United States, is located in the Johnson family cemetery on the grounds of the LBJ Ranch near Johnson City, Texas.

The red granite stone, forty-four inches high and thirty-six inches wide, is supported by a concrete base forty-four inches long and twenty-four inches wide and stands beside the graves of his parents and grandparents.

The inscription reads:

LYNDON BAINES JOHNSON
AUGUST 27, 1908
JANUARY 22, 1973
36th PRESIDENT
OF THE
UNITED STATES OF AMERICA

A replica of the Presidential Seal is carved below.

The Johnson Row in the Beautiful Country Burial Ground

Courtesy of Lyndon B. Johnson Historic Site

"Beneath those rugged elms, that Yew tree's shade,
Where heaves the turf in many a mould'ring heap.
Each in his narrow cell for ever laid,
The rude forefathers of the hamlet sleep."

To the right of President Johnson's grave monument are similar, but smaller stones marking the graves of his parents.

The inscriptions read:

REBEKAH BAINES JOHNSON
1881 — 1958
NONE KNEW THEE BUT TO LOVE THEE
NONE NAMED THEE BUT TO PRAISE

SAM EALY JOHNSON
1877 — 1937
OF PUREST GOLD FROM THE MASTER'S HAND
A MAN WHO LOVED HIS FELLOW MAN

One red granite stone marks the graves of President Johnson's grandfather and grandmother.

The inscription on the stone reads:

S. E. JOHNSON
BORN NOV. 12, 1838
DIED FEB. 25, 1915

ELIZA JOHNSON
BORN JUNE 24, 1849
DIED JAN. 30, 1917

"HE GIVETH HIS BELOVED SLEEP"

The base is inscribed:

FATHER — MOTHER

View Toward President Johnson's Birthplace

Courtesy of Lyndon B. Johnson Historic Site

"Far from the madding crowd's ignoble strife,
Their sober wishes never learned to stray;
Along the cool seqester'd vale of life
They kept the noiseless tenour of their way."

Courtesy of Lyndon B. Johnson Historic Site

Statue of President Johnson on the Road to the Cemetery

The heroic statue of Lyndon Baines Johnson, U.S. President November 22, 1963 — January 20, 1969, stands on a terrace overlooking the Pedernales River, on the road to the family cemetery.

The extended right arm pointing toward the East may be symbolic of the progressive programs of the Great Society:

> Space Exploration
> Poverty Alleviation
> Environmental Protection
> Education Opportunities for All
> Civil Rights — Conflict in Vietnam
> Health Care for the Elderly

The initial letters of the programs of the Great Society are acronymous with LBJ's first position as teacher of SPEECH at the Sam Houston High School.

> "Th' applause of list'ning senates to command,
> The threats of pain and ruin to despise,
>   To scatter plenty o'er a smiling land,
> And read their history in a nation's eyes.
>
> "There at the foot of yonder nodding beech,
> That wreathes its old fantastic roots so high,
>   His listless length at noon tide would he stretch
> And pore upon the brook that babbles by."

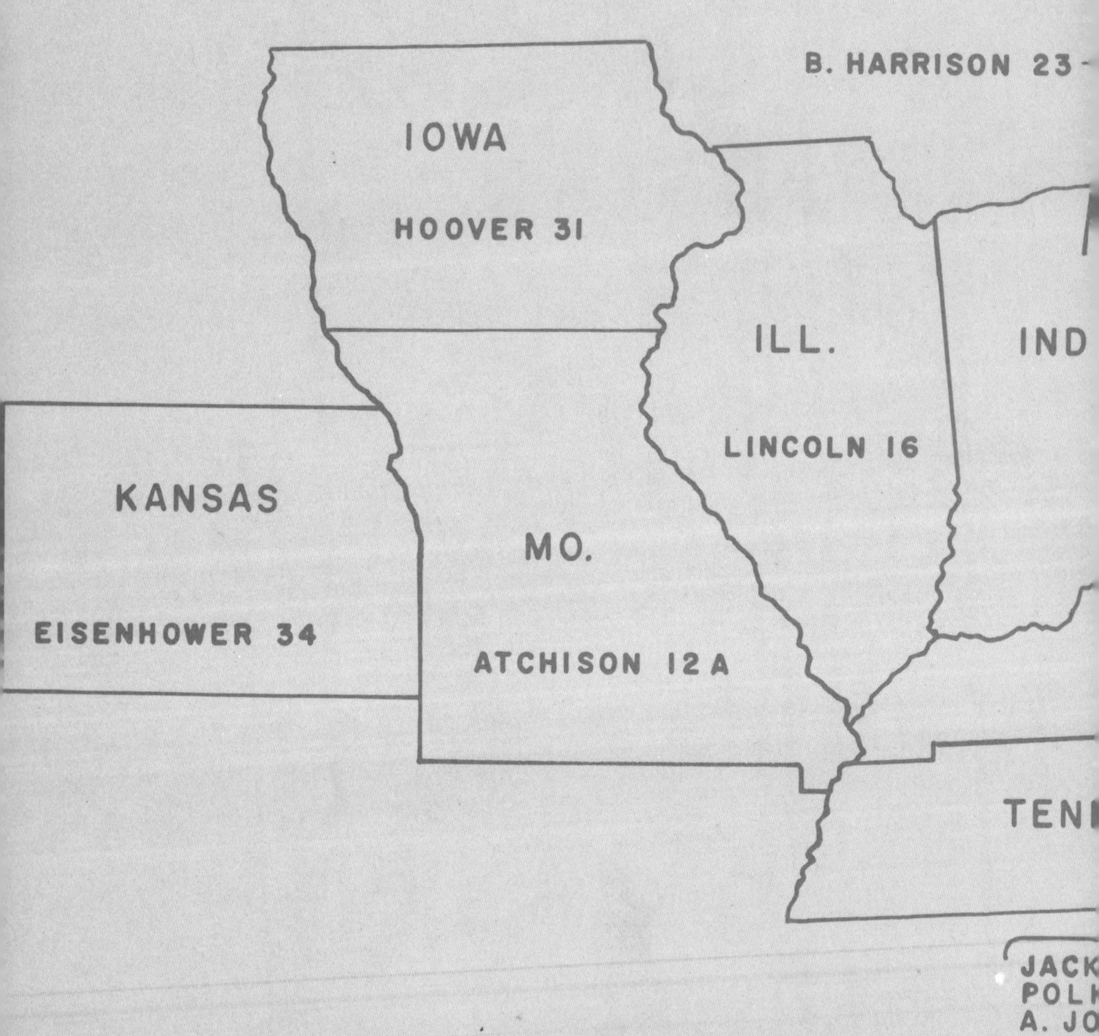
B. HARRISON 23-
IOWA
HOOVER 31
ILL.
IND
LINCOLN 16
KANSAS
MO.
EISENHOWER 34
ATCHISON 12 A
TEN
JACK
POLK
A. JO

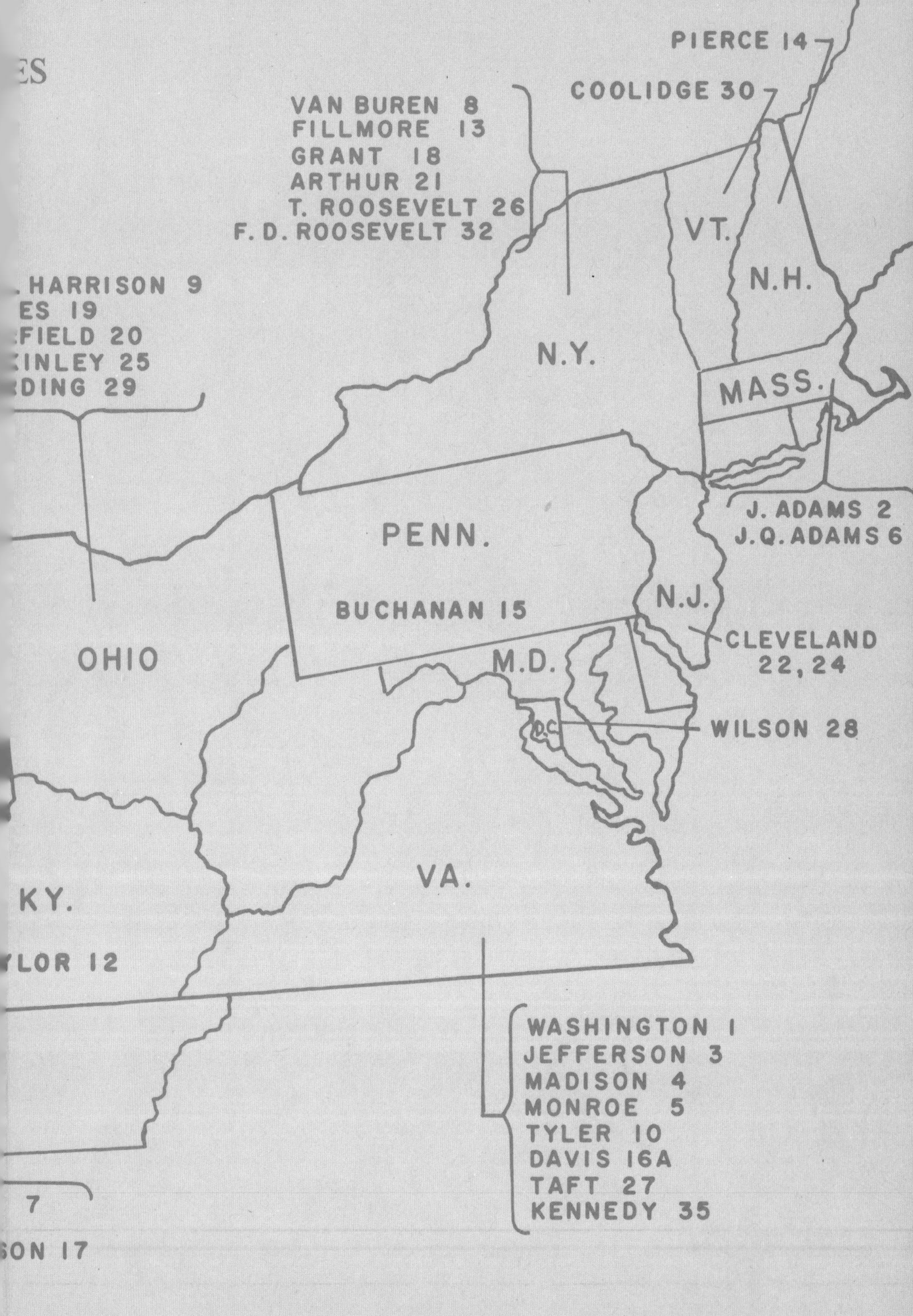
ES
PIERCE 14
COOLIDGE 30
VAN BUREN 8
FILLMORE 13
GRANT 18
ARTHUR 21
T. ROOSEVELT 26
F. D. ROOSEVELT 32
VT.
N.H.
HARRISON 9
ES 19
FIELD 20
INLEY 25
DING 29
N.Y.
MASS.
J. ADAMS 2
J. Q. ADAMS 6
PENN.
BUCHANAN 15
N.J.
OHIO
CLEVELAND
22, 24
M.D.
WILSON 28
D.C.
VA.
KY.
LOR 12
WASHINGTON 1
JEFFERSON 3
MADISON 4
MONROE 5
TYLER 10
DAVIS 16A
TAFT 27
KENNEDY 35
7
SON 17